IGNITING A NEW GENERATION
OF BELIEVERS

Ministry for the Third Millennium

Edited by Lyle E. Schaller

IGNITING A NEW GENERATION OF BELIEVERS

RICHARD P. SCHOWALTER

ABINGDON PRESS / Nashville

IGNITING A NEW GENERATION OF BELIEVERS

Copyright © 1995 by Abingdon Press

This book is printed on recycled, acid-free paper.

Library of Congress Cataloging-in-Publication Data

Schowalter, Richard P.
    Igniting a new generation of believers / Richard P. Schowalter, Jr. : edited by Lyle E. Schaller.
        p.   cm.
    Includes bibliographical references.
    ISBN 0-687-01492-1 (alk. paper)
    1. Church growth.   2. Church work with children.   3. Church work with teenagers.
4. Church work with families.   I. Schaller, Lyle E.   II. Title.
BV652.25.S37 1996
254'.5—dc20   95-38636
                                                                          CIP

Scripture quotations are from the New Revised Standard Version Bible, copyright 1989, by the Division of Christian Education of the National Council of the Churches of Christ in the United States of America. Used by permission.

95 96 97 98 99 00 01 02 03 04—10 9 8 7 6 5 4 3 2 1

MANUFACTURED IN THE UNITED STATES OF AMERICA

CONTENTS

FOREWORD

What is the one universal characteristic of every Christian congregation on the North American continent as we prepare for a new millennium? While these churches differ greatly in doctrine, in polity, and in local traditions, they share one common characteristic. What is that one common characteristic?

During the next several decades, every member will do one or more of the following: (1) move away or (2) drop out or (3) die. That means every Christian congregation has two choices as it plans for the third millennium. One option is to expect to dissolve or to merge into another congregation some time during the twenty-first century. The other option is to identify, reach, serve, attract, assimilate, and disciple a new constituency.

A short term alternative that is being followed by at least one-half of all the Protestant congregations on this continent is to drift passively into the future while watching the members grow older and fewer in numbers.

This book offers a far more exciting, relevant, and challenging option. That option is to reach new generations of people with the good news of Jesus Christ.

For at least a few more years, the old ways of doing ministry will be adequate to reach perhaps one-fourth of the churchgoers born after World War II. The churches that are reaching the other three-fourths have discovered that new wineskins are required. This book is about the design of those new wineskins.

Where do you begin? The best answer is to do as this book does, begin with ministries with children, their parents, and their siblings. Three of the key concepts in this ministry are identified by the words relevance, experience, and excitement. In the first chapter, Pastor Schowalter describes in practical detail how this can be accomplished.

For many churches, the most disruptive discovery of recent years has been that few of today's teenagers were born back in the 1950s or 1960s. A new generation of teenagers arrived with the babies born in the post-1969 era. What worked so well in youth ministries in the 1960s or 1970s or early 1980s no longer works. Why? One reason is those approaches to youth ministries were designed by adults for an adult dominated world in which most teenagers looked to adults for wisdom, knowledge, leadership, affirmation, expertise, authority, and guidance. That world has almost disappeared and exists today largely in the heads of people age twenty-eight and over.

Today teenagers look primarily and largely to their peers for leadership. The second chapter of this book introduces, explains, and details the concept of peer leadership.

The contemporary emphasis on "family values" has renewed interest in the churches in family ministries. The third chapter is filled with practical suggestions on how to translate that interest into reality.

For far too many people, one of the most divisive issues of recent years has been to choose between evangelism or social action and social ministries. That is a false dichotomy. This is most obvious in those congregations that today are reaching large numbers of adults and teenagers born after 1955. These generations seek a worshiping community that *both* nurtures their personal religious journey *and* challenges them to be engaged in doing outreach ministries. In the fourth chapter, the author describes how this is being done. Doing, witnessing, and proclaiming are compatible concurrent themes in hands-on outreach ministries.

Nearly every congregation wants to reach younger generations. Why does it not happen? For many churches, the point of greatest frustration is in worship. Older members treasure the traditional and predictable forms of worship. Many believe a presentation style is the norm. In the fifth chapter the author makes the point that worship must be both relevant and welcoming and also suggests how that can be accomplished.

Perhaps the one area of ministry that combines more hopes, frustrations, high expectations, and disappointments is small groups. In the sixth chapter, Pastor Schowalter begins by separating the facts from the fictions. One of the most disappointing fictions is that the creation and nurture of a network of small groups is low cost, easy, self-perpetuating, and a guaranteed road to numerical growth. In addition to refuting these myths, the author offers a carefully designed and comprehensive strategy for this approach to ministry.

What is the key variable in predicting the future of a particular congregation? The community context? The denominational affiliation? The current size? Demographic trends? Real estate? The quality and relevance of worship? The date when that congregation was founded? The financial base? The program? The ethnic heritage? The attendance in the Sunday school?

While all these factors are relevant variables, the key variable will be the ability of that congregation to identify, reach, serve, assimilate, and disciple a new constituency. That is the theme of this book. What is the key variable in being able to do that? The answer to that question is leadership, this the focus of the final chapter. For many pastors, this will be the most valuable chapter in this volume.

This is another volume in the series *Ministry for the Third Millennium*. The threefold volume of this series is to combine theory and practice with a strong future orientation. That describes this book. The author is a highly competent practitioner who is able to conceptualize both the why and the how. These gifts are combined here with the focus on reaching younger generations of people. That requires being (a) faithful to the gospel and (b) responsive to the needs these younger generations bring to the church. That explains why this book has been written for this series.

Lyle E. Schaller
Naperville, Illinois

INTRODUCTION:

EXPERIENCE AND EXCITEMENT

It is time for a church revival! The gods of our modern culture are proving to be false gods. Materialism has an insatiable appetite, dominating time and energy, leaving only false promises of joy and fulfillment. Entertainment drains our dollars and plays with our emotions, but our problems remain. The seekers today are not asking the biblical question "What must I do to be saved?" The question being asked today is "What must I do to survive?" The church must answer the "survival" question for revival to take place. New answers must be found to answer new questions. It's not time for a "good old-fashioned" church revival. It's time for a new revival, suited for the church in the twenty-first century. God's Holy Spirit is never boring. God's Holy Spirit is relevant and dynamic. God's Holy Spirit must be listened to today, so that the gospel of Jesus Christ can answer the yearning, searching questions of a new generation of believers.

The church is growing and alive in some areas, while it is dying and stagnant in others. Some churches are experiencing phenomenal growth in numbers, while others are withering while graying.

Other churches are experiencing less growth in numbers, but they are feeling a resurgence in the quality of their ministry and a corresponding excitement among their members to reach out to others. For some churches, new members go out the back door more quickly than they can be brought through the front door. For others, not only are new members becoming active, but more so, present inactive members are becoming reactivated. Some churches are in a survival mode with a majority of the efforts and dollars spent in self-serving endeavors, with little or no effort directed to the unchurched or underchurched within the community or the inactive or the new member within the church. Other churches are breaking down the barriers, reaching out to their community and nurturing their members while providing their growth and maturity in Christ.

This book proposes to provide a sense of urgency in looking at our church's ministry in a new and fresh way with the hope that:

1) the *unchurched* of the community may seek the church's expression of faith because of its relevance and effectiveness.

2) the *inactive* within the church may be challenged to participate in new directions for ministry.

3) the *new member* may be assimilated into the church's ministry so that a faithful commitment is generated and firmly established on a long-term basis.

4) the faithful member will be inspired to new visions of ministry.

This book will provide a tool by which the above may be accomplished by the leadership of the church.

This "new and fresh" look at the ministry of the church encompasses the following areas:

1. Children's ministries
2. Youth ministries
3. Family ministries
4. Ministry with the poor
5. Worship and music ministries

6. Large group ministries
7. Small group ministries

One or all of these ministry areas may be in need of a new outlook in a given congregation. The key is the church's self-assessment, followed by the implementation of the suggestions found in each area. You are the church of Jesus Christ. Your church brings together those God has called to be his church in a unified whole. The weak are lifted by the strong, the ignorant are informed by those with understanding, the lax are inspired by the energy of the enthusiastic. Will Rogers said, "Everyone is ignorant, only on different subjects." The challenge for you is to become informed and make a difference in your church. The tools are here. My prayer is that they are useful tools in your hands, empowered by God's Spirit to bring about significant renewal in your church.

This book is a tool that is especially suited for:

1. Church professional staff
2. Church council and other lay leadership
3. Adult and children's ministry educators
4. Evangelism committee
5. Worship and music committee
6. New members class

This is a book designed to help Christians look at themselves and their churches in a new and creative way. God's voice of vision for the church is "See, I am making all things new" (Rev. 21:5). Come Lord Jesus and make my church new through me.

1

CHILDREN'S MINISTRIES THAT MOTIVATE AND EXCITE

Often, Sunday church school lacks excitement. Most of us have forgotten all of our Sunday school teachers—all of them, except perhaps a few. Were those few memorable teachers exceptional teachers? Were our only memorable Sunday school teachers better at what they did than the others? The answer is often "no" to both questions. Most memorable about our Sunday school experience is not so much the content of what teachers taught, but rather their excitement or passion in teaching it, and how they affected our hearts, the seat of our emotions, with that passion.

It is often said that the Christian faith is not as much taught as it is caught. We remember the excitement in their voices when they talked about the love of Jesus. We remember teachers who read the Scriptures with anticipation and hunger. Often, as children, we may not have been too sure about our faith in Jesus, but we knew without a doubt that faith in Jesus was important to our most effective teachers.

Our children are often a reflection of the adult world that creates them. Adults may not realize that they, too, are looking for excitement in their church experience, but they do realize that they are looking for a church that has a positive impact on their lives. No longer is a sense of obligation enough to motivate church participation. The church must produce.

The church must become a positive influence in the lives of its members. The church must answer a key question of our time; "What must I do to survive?" The church must prove that its ministry improves the quality of life for its community. Now, as never before, churches that are failing to positively influence the lives of its members, who fail to improve the quality of life for its community, are dying. Stand on the church roof and shout, "Give me a shovel to help!" Let's bury the ineffective practices, let's seek higher goals, let's fulfill the ministry of Jesus Christ—or quit pretending to be followers of the resurrected Christ.

Adults are often too sophisticated to simply seek a church that is exciting. But where churches change and influence lives, where churches make a difference in the world we live in, there is tangible excitement. We offer you tools and insights to positively influence lives and bring a healing, redeeming ministry to the community that surrounds us. Excitement will follow and the church will be renewed.

First we learn from our children's desire for excitement, which is a by-product of various circumstances. We can become excited by an individual who is excited. We can become excited by participation in a group experience. We can become excited by someone who sincerely listens to us and seems to understand us, while others talk at us, not with us. Excitement has many motivations; without it we are teachers, but our students cannot hear. We can only fill the head and not the heart when excitement is missing. Without a heart's commitment to faith through excitement, the head's knowledge will be impotent and ineffective.

How do we excite our children about the faith of Christ? First, let's overcome "boring" classes. Boredom is most often a by-product of repetition. And repetition of style is far more boring than repetition of content. For example, some professors think that college students "learn" when a teacher enters the lecture hall with his head down, speaks for two hours, and then leaves. We might even later believe that we learned a lot, if we did what was required to get the grade or the degree. But we have a marvelous capacity to deny painful experiences, to rationalize that the tedium of a two-hour lecture was worth the ticket. Back in the Sunday school class, where students assemble voluntarily, the teacher eventually discards bloated content, if there is too much of it, or if it is apparently irrelevant to the needs of the children. But, then lacking suitable content, the teacher often slips into a rut—and then even the content is sacrificed. This apathetic syndrome results in a problem in many Sunday schools that perpetuate a repetition of a teaching style that is information-centered and not excitement-centered, a style that is centered within the head and not the heart. What good is it to be able to recite the Ten Commandments if we fail to see the effects of the Ten Commandments day by day? When we instill faith in our children, our best tactic is not trying to have them acknowledge with the head that God exists, for even God's enemies "believe" that God exists. A living faith is of the heart. A heart moved in a positive direction is excited. To excite our children, we move their hearts by transforming our Sunday school teaching styles.

No one particular style will fit everyone. Here we identify and discuss four styles. These styles are affected by the observation that children and teens want and appreciate change, or at least rebel at traditional worship styles that are imposed upon them. Most adults want and appreciate what they have come to own as traditional. So we try to teach adults how to appreciate the child's value in creativity and change. Many older adults were taught that communication consists of the transmission of words, either spoken or printed. New generations of children have been taught that communication consists of music, color, visual images, words, motion, change of pace, touching, and loads of emotion.

It may be difficult to change the Sunday school teachers who have been doing it their way for the last twenty years. Thus we wisely avoid imposing a revolutionary change on the Sunday school. It is probably best to pilot a new approach to teaching Sunday school with a new teacher on the staff in only one classroom. Maybe several classrooms would prefer to experiment with several different teaching styles. Plant the seeds, the Lord will give the growth. Move in the areas of least resistance first. Earn the right to be heard by presenting a proven style that has already achieved positive results in reaching younger generations.

Here are several already proven ideas to promote enthusiasm among the children in the Sunday school.

Children's Worship

Excitement is generated by being a part of a large group. A sense of power is generated by singing together, especially when that singing demands participation of not only the voice but also the hands and feet. Is your congregation blessed with Sunday school teachers who can effectively communicate their faith and their relationship with Christ in a contagious and enthusiastic way? Why have that teacher's talent limited to a single classroom when it could be used to address the entire Sunday school in a worship setting? Many children find that they do not know, nor do they appreciate their faith until it s shared. We might use children's worship to allow older Sunday school classes an opportunity to share their faith with younger children through drama, puppets, or song. You will revitalize your Sunday school and make it one of the most powerful sources of evangelism in the church if you include a children's worship experience in the Sunday school.

Choosing a Time for Children's Worship

The first questions to be answered in starting a children's worship are when to have it and for how long. If your church has an education hour for adults and children, with adult worship before and/or after the education hour, consider this schedule.

(1) Have children's worship for the first or even the last twenty minutes of the Sunday school hour. If the building encourages it, offer a third alternative—Sunday school class for twenty minutes—worship twenty minutes—class twenty minutes. The problem with this approach is that it takes time away from the present Sunday school class, and some teachers may object that they cannot get all the work they would like to get done within a shortened time frame. The "problem" for the teachers, however, may be a "blessing" for the children. It is difficult to keep the attention of children for an entire hour. Even for the most skilled and sensitive teachers, the devastation of boredom in a child's mind may be much too persistent and pervasive. With only an emphasis at best on filling the head with ideas and not the heart with passion, it may be argued that the longer, the better. But where the heart is concerned, quality is more important than quantity. It could be argued that the entire lesson is not all of such quality that parts of it might better be eliminated for the sake of quality. It could also be argued that the lessons could be divided in two, and the Sunday school could save half their curriculum budget, which in turn could be invested into the children's worship. The advantage of this option is that variety is offered to the Sunday school experience, and variety is our greatest tool for carving up routine.

(2) If your Sunday school teachers refuse to move and want their sixty or forty-five minutes kept intact, consider another option. Encourage children to worship with their families prior to the Sunday school hour or immediately following the Sunday school hour. Project the expectation that everyone of all ages will be in worship and also in Sunday school. During the service, have a children's sermon where the children can be called to the front of the church, and following the children's sermon, have them dismissed to attend children's worship. This option encourages families to worship together but does not demand that children sit through the adult sermon. This option necessitates that children stay two hours at church or choose between worship and Sunday school. It solves the problem of fallout because of a shortened Sunday

school hour, but it does introduce the problem of a divided house. Some will choose not to attend the children's worship, and that usually includes parents who drop their children at Sunday school and go home or run errands. Others may use the children's worship as a Sunday school substitution and skip the Sunday school hour in favor of worship.

There is also a mechanical problem of how to get the children from children's worship to their Sunday school classes if you choose to have a children's worship preceding the Sunday school hour. Teachers are often busy, parents may or may not even be present, so often another volunteer or even several volunteers need to help children get to their classrooms. We have used this option and with sixty to seventy children in children's worship, from preschoolers to sixth graders, this was our biggest headache, especially when a little one was getting lost almost every Sunday. The transition problem is not as great if the children's worship follows the Sunday school hour. Parents simply pick up their children from Sunday school, parents and children attend worship together, and following the children's sermon the children attend children's worship in another building. When the adult worship is over, parents pick up their children.

(3) It is possible to provide a full hour of children's worship prior to the Sunday school hour. This approach is especially difficult because ages are mixed and older children may be ready for a one hour children's worship, but the younger children would not be. Generally, an hour of children's worship is too long and should only be considered with exceptionally entertaining resources for children. It has been my experience that adults like the idea of worship as a family, but it's too much of a struggle for small children. A short time in adult worship and a short time in children's worship appears to give the best of both worlds. The more music you have, the easier it is to increase the amount of content for that hour.

If the church has an adult worship service at the same time as the Sunday school hour, it is not likely that a children's worship will be very effective prior to the Sunday school hour or following it. A good number of children must attend the children's worship to give the feeling of worship. If only ten to fifteen children attend, there will be too few attending to give the feeling and excitement of corporate worship. The only real option for a church that has simultaneous worship and Sunday school and wants to have children's worship, is to have it during the Sunday school hour. Apologize to teachers for a shortened class time, but when done well, children's worship can motivate our children's faith in ways that are impossible in a classroom setting.

What Does Children's Worship Look Like?

Music is vital to effective children's worship, but of course, leave the hymnal in the sanctuary pew. Music for children must be upbeat in terms of tempo, easy to learn and memorize, and have actions with hands and/or feet that make the songs participatory as well as meaningful. Youth today, for the most part, are not listening to music that they can sing. Most youth music is simply heard but that does not make it nonparticipatory music. The music still demands nonverbal participation.

Children's music that demands verbal and nonverbal participation will be more in keeping with the sensitivities of today's youth. Many would describe these songs as "camp songs." (See the music series entitled *We Sing,* or get a copy of the songbook simply titled *Songs,* published by Songs and Creations, Inc., San Anselmo, California, which has all the old favorites.) Guitar players often have the enthusiasm needed to lead these songs. It is more difficult to find a piano player who can play and lead the songs at the same time. Regardless of which instrument is used to accompany the children's songs, it works best to have someone other than the accompanist lead the songs. A song leader overflowing with enthusiasm and a feel for the songs will make them fun and engaging.

The actions are very important. It is even fun to create your own actions to a song if the song is now being sung without benefit of actions. Assign a class the job of creating the actions for a song and have them teach others. Possibly, the creation could be a new song altogether, or an old song with new lyrics, or just some hand movements to add to the song as is. Let them experiment with other aids to singing such as percussion instruments, or try new forms of songs, like a Christian rap sound.

It is also effective to use a hymn with a new beat or make up actions to a slow-moving hymn and make it into a group dance experience. We have used a Christian marching band with appropriate songs, complete with simple percussion instruments. We have chosen to use appropriate songs for the experience of prayer. Some children love echo songs. We have sung "Humble Thyself," which is wonderfully effective in preparing children for prayer. We all have seen hundreds of giggling, active children settle down and have their mood change dramatically when the lone voice of the song leader begins by singing "Humble thyself in the sight of the Lord," and half the children echo "Humble thyself in the sight of the Lord." "And he" (echoed by children "And he"), "will lift" (echoed "will lift"), "you up" (echoed "you up"). By this time, everyone is in tune with the attitude of prayer and the verse "Sing together in the sight of the Lord" or "Pray together in the sight of the Lord" is, without exception, sung with unity and sensitivity.

Prayer is vital to accomplish effective children's worship. Again, variety will be the biggest weapon in defeating boredom, but perhaps equally important is relevance. The key is variety in style and relevance in content.

Variety in prayer style takes many creative avenues. As mentioned, prayer through simple songs is a powerful tool in making worship unified. Little voices praying through song is a good way to introduce and prepare for a spoken prayer. A litany of prayer is also effective with children. Ask each child to pray: "The Lord has given me (*an object or person*)," and let each child fill in the blank with a personal blessing. After each personal prayer of thankfulness, have the entire group respond: "Thank you, Jesus." Or the litany could be: "The person God has given me to love is (*name*)," and the entire group could respond: "God is good." Create your own litany of prayer, or assign Sunday school classes or individuals to create their own prayers. Have children draw their prayers with colorful scenes and let them lead the group in prayer centered around each scene. Specific words could be recited or merely let the prayer scene speak for itself as each child prays in silence, led by the visual suggestion of the drawing. Adults can lead prayer in children's worship by having the children repeat short phrases of a lengthy prayer.

A prayer technique we have used to solicit children's prayers is what we call the "popcorn prayer." Everyone sits in a circle holding hands. Usually the adult leader begins by praying a short prayer. When the prayer is completed, the hand being held on either the left or the right side is squeezed, which signals their turn to pray out loud if they wish. If they want to pray, the squeeze is their signal to begin. If they do not wish to pray out loud (it is explained that everyone is praying silently the entire time), then they simply pass on the squeeze. The prayer is complete when the squeeze has made its way around the circle. The benefit of the popcorn prayer is that everyone has a specific opportunity to pray, each prayer ends with a squeeze (ending a prayer can be the most awkward part of a spoken prayer.) The sense of community built with prayer is very powerful. With older children, the prayer can be used as a tool to have everyone prayed for. Ask everyone to share a personal prayer concern. Have the person on the right or left, depending on the direction of the squeeze around the circle, pray for the prayer concern that was shared by that person.

Relevance in content is best accomplished by offering a time for children to express their prayer concerns. Discuss what prayer is, give examples of types of prayers, and have children write and speak prayers in their own words. Use visual aids for prayer and ask the children what they see, notice how they react, and ask what prayerful response they have to the visual aids. A potted flower, a cross, a picture from a magazine, a lighted candle could all be a focus for prayer, but what is seen or experienced should come from the children, in their own words. Often, children are not skilled in verbal communication, so try to use artwork or objects to solicit prayers. Again, we are looking for a variety of style and a relevance of content.

In the presentation of the lesson, parables can be presented as skits by one of the older classes. Other lessons can be represented by drawings made by younger classes. Children love to be given an audience for their efforts. Children's worship can provide that audience. Many times, we do not know what our faith is until we share it. Children's worship can provide the forum for children to share their faith with each other, thereby helping their faith to take shape and grow stronger. There are many other creative ways to present a lesson that are not as commonplace as a skit or a drawing. How about a rap song or the changing of the lyrics of a familiar song to present a lesson? Bring in pets when talking about Jesus the good shepherd and, relate how we must take care of our pets the way Jesus, the good shepherd, takes care of his sheep. Dance, use motions to familiar songs or sign language, choral reading, clay, playing a game. The list goes on of possible ways children individually, or in classes, can present the scripture lesson or theme for children's worship.

The key is in both finding the talented adults who can do a good job presenting a lesson for the children, or in letting the children take the responsibility themselves. It affirms children's families to have parents come in to explain their occupations or careers in terms of how God uses them to be a benefit to others and share their faith. Bring in professionals who are not parents to share their faith with the children. From athletes to nurses, from teachers to receptionists, the adult can model the Christian life by explaining how their faith influences their careers and jobs. In a pinch, the children could even watch a wide variety of cartoon videos that depict a biblical lesson or story. Some are more dramas rather than cartoons, but they, too, are effective. Puppets are powerful tools in getting the attention of children and presenting a lesson. There are also clown and magician ministries that make an effective presentation of gospel themes. The list goes on. Never settle in for too long on any one style of presentation. Children love change. The good today will not be the good for tomorrow. Remember, the enemy for children's ministry is boredom. Children's worship that defeats boredom is both participatory and constantly changing, creative and dynamic. There are many resources to accomplish the above, but the fault is most often an unwillingness to implement the resources available.

Reward and Gift-Centered Children's Ministry

Many of us would make a distinction between rewards for behavior and rewards for character. Children should not be rewarded for character traits. Children should be rewarded for efforts and accomplishments. For example, it is not appropriate to reward a child for telling the truth. Being truthful should be its own reward, in terms of enriched character. In the same way, children should not be given incentives for being faithful to God, no matter what kind of behavior that faithfulness to God demands. We should not consider prayer a criterion for rewards and incentives. Prayer is to be expected as a Christian practice. It is ridiculous to reward children for their prayers. On the other hand, children must be encouraged to have their Christian character translate into Christian behavior. Jesus makes no apologies about stating that Christian conduct will be rewarded. Look at the beatitudes ("Blessed are . . .") all imply rewards for Christian conduct. Jesus is the vine; we are the branches. To be cemented to the vine is to bear fruit; to be disconnected is to whither and die. Jesus said, "You will know them by their fruit." A good tree produces good fruit. We would be missing the point to deny children the fruit of their labors. The scriptural principle of sowing and reaping applies here. We will reap what we sow; if we fail to sow we will fail to reap. Rewards and incentives teach our children the principle of sowing and reaping that will be of great benefit to them spiritually, socially, emotionally, relationally, mentally, and physically. Our children must learn the difference between rewards and benefits of Christian behavior, and the free gift of God's salvation based on the character trait of faith. We all need to learn the distinction.

If you can get beyond this psychological stumbling block, you will find that children respond with enthusiastic joy to a program that names the benefits of enthusiastic participation. The program must be presented with wisdom and sensitivity, but where it is done well, children will respond in positive ways that could not be accomplished otherwise. The younger the child, the more powerful tangible incentives will motivate. As children grow older, tangible incentives must be replaced with internal motivations, such as praise and leadership roles. This will be addressed in the next chapter.

We encouraged the creation of an incentive-based children's ministry at St. Luke's Lutheran Church in Bloomington, Minnesota. We called the ministry "God's Gifts," and although it could be used on a Sunday morning, we chose to offer the program during the week, on Thursday evenings. We did so because the material was being piloted and we did not feel that we could jump into the Sunday school of almost 200 children with a program that was in the process of development. The program consisted of four parts. First, we opened with children's music and singing. Then, we had a presentation of the lesson, either through an adult presentation, a skit performed by a group of children, or a children's Christian video. During the presentation, the majority of the leaders would meet together for a review of the material, making plans for the evening or future sessions and prayer. Next, children would meet in designated small groups under the leadership of a "Listener." Kindergarten through first grade were Sprouts, second through third grades were Twigs, and fourth through sixth grades were branches. The job of the Listener was simply to give credit for the work accomplished. The hour and a half would end with refreshments and the children's "store," where children could redeem the tickets they earned for work accomplished. Tickets, which we later changed to a credit card system because we found it too difficult to count out all the tickets every week, were earned for the following:

Memory Verse: two tickets
Questions Answered: two tickets

Parent or Adult Friend's Signature: two tickets

Attendance at Sunday School: two tickets

Attendance at Choir: two tickets

Bring a friend for the first time: five tickets

That friend returns each succeeding time: three tickets

We also gave any new member of God's Gifts fifteen free tickets, but from that first visit on, all other tickets had to be earned by doing the lessons. We ran two ten-week sessions per year. One session was the ten weeks prior to Thanksgiving and the other session was the ten weeks prior to Maundy Thursday. At the end of ten weeks, the total points were accumulated and awards were given for tickets above certain numbers, either Gold, Silver, or Bronze. We took the children's pictures and posted them on a bulletin board with their achieved awards listed. The key to the program's sensitivity was the small group "Listener." All the children received the same lesson. The lesson and memory work was to be done at home with parents or an adult friend. The two points for a signature of the adult friend or parent emphasized that facet.

It was the job of the Listeners to use their best judgment in awarding tickets given the age level of their class and the different abilities of each individual. For example, children in kindergarten may not be able to memorize a lengthy memory verse but they may be able to memorize 1 Peter 5:7: "He cares for you." Often, the Listener for the Sprouts would ask the kindergarten through first graders to simply repeat the Bible verse or a portion of it, either individually or as a group, while a Branch listener for fourth through sixth graders may not only ask each participant to repeat the verse, but also to recite where it is from, book, chapter and verse.

It is also easier to do the memory work one verse at a time in a small group than it is to ask each participant to repeat all the memory verses they know at once. Further, a bright fourth grader may be asked to do more than a slow sixth grader even though they came from the same class. The children were not jealous. They did not all try to get every point, but the points they earned were rewarded. We usually told the children that a ticket is worth three cents. With ten tickets they could buy something that was worth thirty cents. We found that if we asked for a five to ten dollar registration fee, the costs for God's Gifts could be covered. We also had a "World Hunger Jar" and encouraged the children to give ten percent of their tickets to the world hunger jar, where the tickets would be converted to cash and given to the church's world hunger appeal. We have had children give all their tickets, hundreds of tickets, to world hunger. We have had between fifty and seventy children give as many as 3,000 tickets worth ninety dollars to world hunger.

What is difficult to communicate about the program is the joy and excitement it creates. Our five-year-old daughter jumped on my lap and exclaimed, "Dad, I haven't had any fun today, let's do God's Gifts." An older daughter of ours has had such a positive experience learning from God's Gifts that it has been the single most important factor in her developing from a poor to an average student into an exceptional student at school. Incentives, awards, gifts are effective in working with children. Children love to receive gifts, but more important, children are motivated and excited by their faith in Jesus when a comprehensive and sensitive incentive program is instituted. God's Gifts is a children's program designed to meet children in a way that they can be motivated most effectively and positively. A Sunday school program could do the same. We must encourage our Sunday school teachers accordingly.

A less dramatic incentive program could also be incorporated into the Sunday school. At the end of each Sunday school year, we have gone all-out to put on a Sunday school picnic and carnival. The carnival games are played with a ticket system. In the weeks prior to the carnival, we make it well known that children can earn free tickets to the carnival by their attendance or their accomplishments. If you want to add an evangelistic element, give away tickets to children who bring a school friend to Sunday school the weeks prior to the carnival. Offer free tickets to their guests just for coming to Sunday school and more free tickets to continue to come. The system cannot fail. Children are excited and overjoyed. We have seen attendance at a down time of year increase 10 to 20 percent. Many unchurched children come to Sunday school for the first time.

Deby Schowalter has used an incentive program as director of a kindergarten through second grade children's choir. As children enter they are given two cards. If a child becomes disruptive, is failing to pay attention, or has any other behavior problem, a card is taken away. At the end of the hour, those who have cards left can redeem them for a piece of candy. Prior to the incentive program the choir was out of control, but seldom now does a card have to be taken away. The transformation is amazing.

It should be noted that the older the child, the less effective is a reward or incentive program. Young children are excited and positive toward almost any reward system as long as it is fair. Older children tend to be more motivated by responsibilities and tasks. Thus, the older the child, the less likely the God's Gifts program will be effective. For the older class, the fourth throught sixth graders, we try to give responsibilities to encourage their continued participation and interest. We may ask them to work on a skit or a song to present to the entire group to introduce a lesson. We may ask them to choose the gifts for others from a toy catalogue for the God's Gifts store. We may ask them to run the store or to serve refreshments. They may be asked to pray a prayer or lead the actions to a song. For the most responsible youth, we may ask them to be a listener for two or three of the younger youth. When older youth are given responsibilities, often they respond conscientiously and with a passion that is impressive.

Bob Benedict is the author of God's Gifts, and resources can be ordered by writing to him at 6948 West 105th Street, Bloomington, Minnesota 55438. Another excellent children's ministry program that incorporates incentives is "Good News Bearers."

The Good News Bearers emphasizes four program areas: 1) large group activities for children and families; 2) a weekly program where older youth lead younger youth in performing a Bible-based skit for one another; 3) a children's Bible reading program where children read Bible stories in preparation for a Bible trivia bowl; and 4) the performing of biblical musicals.

The large group activities create excitement and build relationships between families. We went to an all-church hayride and picnic that brought many people together from many walks of life who would never have socialized together under any other circumstance.

The weekly program takes Bible stories and divides them up into several skits. The children work on practicing the skits, then performing them for one another. The skits are directed by older youth who have the designation of a T.I.M. or Teen In Mission. The program boasts that there is often minimal retention of a story that is read to a child, but when a child performs the story as a skit for others, there is almost 100 percent retention of the details.

The Bible reading program is designed for parents to read stories to their children or parents to verify that their children have read the stories on their own. When a certain number of stories have been read over a designated time, the children participate in a Bible trivia bowl, with rewards and recognition for all the participants and something special for the winners.

The biblical musicals are more encouraged than given specific instructions for, but I, too, recommend their use. The greatest benefit to a child in being part of a musical production is that it creates a lasting memory.

The Good News Bearers is written by Tim Strommen and can be ordered through the Augsburg Youth and Family Institute, 2211 Riverside Avenue, Minneapolis, Minnesota 55454-1351.

Intergenerational Children's Ministry

God's Gifts and Good News Bearers include another major emphasis that is also an exciting way to minister to children. Parents or an adult friend are vitally involved in the programs. The children are asked to do their reading or memory work at home and answer the questions on the lesson with an adult, most often a parent.

American Protestants have a long and strong tradition of separating generations for educational purposes within the church. This is done with the understanding that education involves communication of knowledge, and that different generations must receive in their own way, given their own dispositions and abilities. However, education is more than the passing on of knowledge or content. Like the Sunday school teacher whose lessons we cannot remember, but whose commitment and dedication to faith stand out, so we need to realize that faith is a product of both the sharing of knowledge and the imitation of human practices or disciplines. Knowledge without modeling is an intellectual experience that may or may not have an impact on our lives. Knowledge that is modeled has a far greater influence on our lives because it is knowledge that lives.

Parents need to teach and model their faith, but also children need to teach and model faith from their own perspective. Together, adults and children will find enrichment, learning, and the mutual discovery of God's Spirit. Here are some ideas for intergenerational ministry:

(1) Sunday school does not have to be the same experience each Sunday. For example, Sundays on holiday weekends like Labor Day or Memorial weekend, the Sunday following the Fourth of July or the Sunday between Christmas and New Years all lend themselves to giving Sunday school teachers a break and bringing children and parents together in one place for an intergenerational learning event. This event could begin with singing and then a theme could be introduced. The theme could be introduced through some kind of special entertainment, like a singing group, puppets, drama, or the like. After the introduction of the theme, break the large group into small groups, mixing children and adults. Have the small groups discuss a question or an issue. Create an art project or a skit. It is amazing and fun to see children working together with adults of all ages on an assigned task. These special holiday Sundays are looked forward to in our congregation and people attend who may never attend any other kind of learning experience.

(2) One of our most exciting and growing intergenerational events is the Advent Family Fair. At this fair, family groups, singles or seniors come to make an Advent log or wreath the evening of the first Sunday of Advent. The fair is prepared for by displaying a replica of the Advent log or wreath for two Sundays before the event, and encouraging family groups to sign up to bring something to a potluck to be held just prior to "log making," as well as collecting a fee for the materials needed to create their own log or wreath. Materials needed include: four candles, plastic poinsettia blooms and holly, ribbons, and the logs or wreaths. Cut evergreen branches and collect pine cones that will also be made available. A family devotional book is bought, or one could be created from the Sunday school classes. The fair starts with a potluck, families then create their Advent log or wreath and the evening ends with everyone lighting their first candle and doing the first devotion together. Add a song or two, end by singing "Silent Night" and you have the ingredients of a fantastic evening. We have found that families who have never done devotions before will faithfully do them together when they have a focal point that they have labored together to create.

(3) It is often difficult to get families to attend a weekend retreat together, but for those who do attend, it can be a yearly winner. The key to a successful family retreat is variety. Offer times when families can work together on a project, then each family can explain and present their project to the retreat as a whole. Try to have a time when adults can spend time together and facilitate discussions on family issues. While the adults are together, recruit older youth to spend time with the younger children. The older youth should be given an appropriate gift or payment for their efforts to supervise the children. Worship is a good time to have each family make a presentation to the group in the form of some art work, a skit, a song or a story from their family experiences. Encourage a time for family devotions in the evening and offer enough free time to allow for unstructured interactions. Even a family game time is often both fun and meaningful. The family

retreat bandwagon often starts out small, but we have found that it creates a faithful core of participants.

(4) Grandpa and Grandma Ministry. Often there is significant desire among older adults to be with children, but the opportunities are rare within our society for that kind of interaction. Not only can teens minister to the "shut-ins" who are trapped by their frail bodies into a solitary existence in an apartment or a nursing home, but older adults with more mobility can offer significant ministry with children. A surrogate grandparent or "adopt-a-grandchild" program is a winner for everyone involved. Solicit participants, kick off the program with a party, and recommend weekly contact. Have periodic events where the pairs are invited. At times, there is a hesitation by senior adults to lead a group or teach a class, but more often, older adults are able and willing helpers. They can usually do more than they first imagined and, with supervision, the generation gap can provide a witness for all involved to discover. If a Sunday school or preschool is connected to the church, involve older adults as volunteer helpers. Have older adults sponsor youth to go on a workcamp or trip, and make sure the youth both thank their adult sponsor and take the time to report on the event to them. Perhaps turn to grandmothers and grandfathers to deliver the children's sermon. Recruit older members as tutors for the neighborhood elementary school children. You will find this a powerful tool in reaching unchurched families living next to the church. The schools welcome this community cooperation.

(5) The most popular small group ministry we promote is an intergenerational Bible study for families or singles, with or without children. The church is too often guilty of separating families for the sake of fellowship and ministry. If the church is ever going to be a force to strengthen our families, it must bring families together around events, groups, and mission. The intergenerational Bible study brings people of all ages together in homes for Bible study, usually for an hour and a half. The time together begins with a children's devotion, where a lesson is read and children are asked questions, both about the lesson and about how the lesson applies

to their lives. After fifteen to twenty minutes for the children's devotion, the children go to one part of the house for a structured play time while the adults have an in-depth Bible study and discussion. Following the forty to fifty minutes of Bible study for the adults and children's playtime, everyone comes together for prayer. Children and adults share their requests; many are willing to speak their prayers at the prayer time, which is open for anyone to pray aloud. There is a beauty in hearing the prayers of children. It is a good idea to light a candle as a focal point and let the child willing to lead a prayer blow out the candle. You will have lots of children eager to pray.

These are great groups to serve as organizers for family evenings or events. Whether the Advent Fair, a concert, a potluck, a talent show, a puppet ministry, or a craft project, the intergenerational Bible study group can serve as the organizer and power base or nucleus for these family events. From these events, which draw a larger audience, new intergenerational groups may be formed. These events provide a great service to the church and the project they sponsor provides a sense of pride and purpose for each group to rally around and be proud of.

(6) Do your Sunday school teachers have a hard time getting substitutes? We tell our Sunday school teachers to call parents of the students as substitute teachers in their class. It works wonderfully. We promote the idea of using our God's Gifts materials at home, instead of coming to the church an additional evening each week. We call it "God's Gifts II," and we simply distribute God's Gifts materials to parents, asking them to both do the lesson and give credit or rewards for the work completed. In God's Gifts II, the church only provides materials—everything else is accomplished in the home where they are free to modify the program any way they see fit. We have started an adult confirmation class meeting at the same time that confirmation instruction is taking place for the youth. This makes it convenient for parents to have adult education while their youth have confirmation, and with the

coordination of the lessons, parents can learn the same material their youth are learning to stimulate conversation at home.

These are just a few ideas with the same principle! Bring children and youth together with their parents to promote mutual learning.

Adult Models and Experiential Learning

Some of us remember going through confirmation for three years with lots of memory work and assignments and the dreaded "public examination" where everyone had to stand up and recite a portion of the catechism and answer questions. The requirements did not hurt, but today we must question their value, especially in comparing the time spent to the desired result of faith development. The greatest lift to a youth's faith development most often occurs at a camp or a retreat. One of the teachers of our youth Bible studies asked twenty youth what the most meaningful spiritual growth experience of their life had been. Of the twenty youth asked this question, eighteen replied that it was their camp experience. A camp or retreat allows youth to experience their faith and not only learn of their faith.

Children also should learn a gospel that walks and talks and has flesh and blood. The stories from the Bible are interesting, but they really don't apply until they are experienced. Children experience faith in relationship to people who live their faith. The question is how can our children get to know adult models of faith?

Retreats for children are a good idea. Many children will not have parents willing to come to family camp. The alternative is to bring children to a grade school camp with as many adult volunteers as possible. It is a stretch for Sunday school teachers to experience their class on a retreat, rather than a classroom. Retreats are a time to share lives together, where the classroom tends to share only thoughts. Lives teach the heart of faith. The knowledge of faith is best learned in a classroom, but faith is more than the accumulation of knowledge.

A wonderful opportunity to bring adults and children together and to share their faith stories is at first communion instruction. Here, young children come to learn about the sacrament that brings the presence of God, literally the touch of God, into their lives. What better place is there to have parents share their faith with their children? The key is to encourage self-disclosure and vulnerability. Faith is not having all the right answers. Often faith is the struggle with doubts, the admission of weaknesses. Give assignments to take home for first communion instruction. Have parents and children discover their faith together.

Another teaching tool, along these same lines, is a hands-on, interactive station approach to learning. It is one thing to be taught the significance of Jesus' crucifixion, it is quite another thing to sit at a table with a lit candle, a spike the size that may have been driven into Jesus' hands and feet, a replica of the crown of thorns, and a vivid picture of the crucifixion to ponder and explore. We can model events or even parables if tangible replicas and representations of those events are provided and children are allowed to touch and explore.

This type of hands-on, explorative learning can be found in a program called: "The Catechism of the Good Shepherd." This is a Roman Catholic program patterned after the Montessori schooling concepts of "self-teaching." The promotional material explains, "The catechite role (adult teacher) is to prepare the environment and to make presentations that 'call forth' the child's response rather than 'pour in' information. The adult is a co-wonderer with the child as they together enjoy meditating on the questions generated by the Scripture with the prepared environment (learning stations) as a developmental aid."

I will never forget a song sung in the Christian musical, "The Witness," by Jimmy and Carol Owens, that we performed on a youth choir tour. The song was a crucifixion song, sung by Mary, Jesus' mother. What made the song so powerful was not only that it was a beautiful song, but the music was literally punctuated by the sound of a hammer striking a large stake. The ringing of that sound, filling the air, did more than anything else to place us all back at the crucifixion. High school and college youth cried night after night, performance after performance, with that striking sound filling the air.

If we can experience our faith, our faith will live and be much more powerful than simply learning about our faith. Whether that faith is to be modeled by a person or experienced on a retreat, at an interactive station or other event, seek the higher good for children and give them opportunities for experiential learning.

2

YOUTH ARE
THE FUTURE CHURCH NOW

Youth ministry for teens must be developed differently from children's ministry. Children are motivated by tangible awards and gifts like prizes and certificates. Youth, for the most part, judge these same awards and gifts as cheap and unappealing. This is a developmental change that occurs gradually from the late elementary years and into the teenage years. With older children, beginning at ages ten to twelve years, motivations will be more internal and relational. A gift will not motivate an older child or youth to read a Bible story, but they will go to a Bible study where they can make new friends and increase the intimacy between existing friends. A certificate of appreciation will not appeal to them, but helping the helpless and making a difference in the lives of others will appeal to them.

The teen years are ripe for evangelism efforts because of their striving for independence. The church of the past was characterized by parents bringing their children to church kicking and screaming. The church of the twenty-first century will be characterized by children bringing their parents to church kicking and screaming. If the future parent refuses to come, then their teens will come by themselves.

A powerful tool for ministry in the church of the third millennium will be peer ministry. Youth peer ministry is already a proven tool.

Youth Peer Ministry Program

Peer ministry has two distinct features. First, it is a mutual ministry, and second, it is ministry that shares weaknesses, fears, doubts, faults, and troubles—rather than wisdom, knowledge, authority, or expertise. Peer ministry is mutual ministry in that the minister expects to learn as well as teach, expects to receive as well as give, expects to be loved and cared for as well as to be loving and caring. Peer ministry is relational ministry, but more than that, peer ministry puts the minister and the recipient of the ministry on the same level. There may be differences in age or economic background or education or a number of other variables, but peer ministry is primarily an equality of attitude, where external variables are discounted and the equality of attitude causes two people in ministry to minister to each other. One may be trained to initiate and nurture the peer ministry relationship, but the fact remains that the focus of the ministry is to learn from each other in mutual ministry.

Youth are very receptive to peer ministry, perhaps because they are testing their own freedom and liberty before adulthood. We have all heard the term "peer pressure" when describing the world of youth. "Peer pressure" need not always be negative. Certainly our school system, which throws all our youth together for the main part of their daily experience, makes peer pressure a constant reality; but peer ministry can make that reality a very positive one. Youth peer ministry takes the given peer pressure that our youth are surrounded by in our society and focuses that "pressure" in constructive and positive avenues. Youth are generally more willing than their adult counterparts to share weaknesses, doubts, and fears because those feelings are often on the surface of their lives and not buried by years of repressing feelings and the defense mechanisms that deal with them.

Peer ministry prevents youth leadership burnout because it takes youth seriously, as powerful ministers in and of themselves. Most youth leaders are caught in an entertainment relationship with their youth, and the church simply cannot compete with the trillions of dollars that are pumped into the entertainment and amusement industries. Though we are convinced that our ministry must be playful and exciting, we must ask ourselves: "What ministry is being accomplished through entertainment?" "What ministry value is there in roller-skating?" Certainly there is "Christian entertainment," especially musically, but is that effective ministry for the small congregation with few resources? The church should get back into the business it is called to accomplish by God, namely, the proclamation of the gospel in Christ. It is a subtle, yet demeaning insult to our youth if we conclude that they should be entertained and amused to keep them active in the church. Would it not be, on the other hand, a tremendous compliment and boost to our youth's self-image to convey to them that they have what it takes to be effective and sensitive ministers to one another? When youth minister to one another, more ministry is accomplished because there are more involved in the ministry. By being a minister to ministers, the youth director or pastor can accomplish more ministry with less effort. Youth ministry burnout is a product of having youth directors and pastors spend endless time and effort trying to entertain their youth while not being able to establish meaningful ministry relationships with so many under their care. Having the ministry goal of an in-depth relationship, we can only effectively minister to ten to twelve youth, the average size of most youth ministries. However, if those ten to twelve can be trained to minister to another ten to twelve each, then the ministry has grown to over 100.

Mutual Youth Ministry may not easily include 100, but it could handle that kind of growth without stretching the youth director, lay leader, or pastor in every direction. Youth peer ministry can work just as effectively in a small congregation as a large one. In a small congregation aim for two peer ministers, ministering to ten to twenty. In larger congregations, the same ratios apply with more youth peer ministers.

Begin with prayer. Peer ministry is founded on the principle that each believing Christian has an active role to play in the church and its mission. That role is empowered by God's Spirit. If the Spirit is the moving force, prayer is the means to activate the force. Peer ministry is not ordinary people doing the extraordinary work of God, but the extraordinary Spirit of God doing the work of God through ordinary people. Prayer is the vehicle that makes God's people ministers, and prayer will keep the ministry of God's people directed and empowered by God's Spirit.

Prayer from the youth's perspective is an education in itself. One of the purposes of peer ministry is to share fears, weaknesses, and troubles, rather than wisdom, strengths and accomplishments. Prayer is most satisfying to the spiritual development of the believer when it arises from the vulnerability of expressed fears, the humility of expressed weaknesses, and the supplication of expressed troubles. Youth are eager, in a safe environment, to lay open their lives to one another. Times of prayer allow defenses to be quickly stripped away, leaving the youth vulnerable, humble, and supplicating as a result. Youth seldom have the sophistication for flowery, refined prayer, impressive in its beauty and poetry. Often prayer is the first major step in establishing the peer ministry relationship. The ability to pray in a group is a strong indication of the youth who should be encouraged to become peer ministers. The willingness to pray in a group indicates an openness to spiritual growth and an expressed vulnerability that is essential in the youth peer minister.

Often, the youth who are best suited for peer ministry are the "average" youth. On the one hand, youth who are at risk often do not have an interest in church activities in general. On the other hand, youth who are very talented and hard-working are often overcommitted at school, are pressured to "rise above their peers," and may have little time to devote to their church. For the most part, the peer ministry team will be made up of talented and hard working youth who are relatively undiscovered. They generally have a self-image concern that has kept them fairly inactive at school, and yet they have a stable enough home life and personal life not to be involved in destructive or unproductive interests.

An optional Bible study for high school youth is a good place to find potential youth peer ministers. Use the Bible study to teach the vision and theology of peer ministry. The themes of these studies could be "Spiritual Maturity" or "Discipleship," but content is not as important as attitude. The youth director, lay leader, or pastor must treat the youth involved as equals. The leader must be willing to learn from the youth—not simply teach them. The youth leader must be vulnerable, open, honest, trusting, and generous with sharing the secrets of his/her own life. Intimacy through self-disclosure is the goal, mutual sharing of thoughts and lives through the study of scripture and prayer is the means. Excellent material for these studies have often come from the publisher of Serendipity Bible studies. All Serendipity material seeks to teach within the context of self-disclosure, and that is the key to youth peer ministry. Serendipity material often is more in tune with youth issues, so that the Serendipity New Testament is particularly effective. In choosing peer ministry material, look for a simple outline with good discussion questions.

Begin the Bible study by affirming the youth for being there and stating your expectations for a small, intimate group. If your group is not small, suggest another time and day so that the group can be split. You are looking for a group of three to seven. Do not soft-pedal the commitment. In fact, lay out the commitment required to be on youth staff. You are not asking them to make an immediate commitment, but express to them that following six to twelve weeks of study, you will take them on a retreat. Following the retreat, you will ask for commitments to become youth peer ministers. The following are suggested youth peer ministry commitments: ·

(1) Daily time for personal prayer and devotions—weekly worship
(2) Weekly Bible study and necessary preparations to lead a Bible study with their own small group
(3) Monthly youth minister meetings
(4) Two youth minister retreats each year—one in the fall and one in midwinter
(5) Elective counseling for confirmation retreats and camp, and counseling senior high trips such as choir tours or work camp and such.

Generally, you are looking for youth that are juniors or seniors in high school, who will be the core of your youth staff. However, these age guidelines may need to be liberalized for the first year or two. The ideal is having juniors and seniors in high school minister to seventh through ninth graders, with the tenth graders having a counselor-in-training (CIT) status. In the program's infancy, how-ever, it may be advisable to have one or two younger youth and/or one or two college age youth. The key is not age but attitude. Do the people involved have a peer ministry attitude, where they: (1) expect not only to teach but to learn, not only to help but also to be helped, and (2) are willing to communicate their own fears, weak-nesses, and faults, not their strengths, wisdom, and accomplish-ments?

Adults who have these attitudes are hard to find, and it is imperative to handpick the adults within the peer ministry group. If the adult is willing to be trained, that in itself will indicate a cooperative attitude. The appropriate adult gravitates to youth in social settings, knows them by name, and is willing to greet them. Generally you are not looking for a disciplinarian of youth but a friend and mentor of youth. This sounds fairly simple and straight-forward, but adults with peer attitudes toward youth are hard to find. The ideal adult to get involved with youth peer ministry is the adult who is eager to understand the youth perspective, who is compli-mentary of youth contributions, and who makes him/herself avail-able to the youth. Youth peer ministry is not just youth ministering to youth of the same age. Most effectively, youth peer ministry is youth who are slightly older ministering to youth who are slightly younger. Because of the developmental stages involved, the best peer ministry takes place with high school youth ministering to junior high youth. Youth peer ministry could also be accomplished with junior high youth ministering to grade school youth, or college-age youth ministering to high school youth, or youth of any age ministering to one another. Youth peer ministry could also occur with an adult ministering to youth, provided that the adult has the peer attitude of mutual sharing and learning with youth—an adult willing and able to share weaknesses, doubts, or failures. Adults must always be outnumbered on a youth peer ministry team, or the youth will take on the assigned cultural roles and not take on the peer ministry role.

Once an initial group of potential youth peer ministers is formed to pray together and learn the biblical perspective of discipleship, along with peer ministry theology, then a retreat for peer ministry candidates can be proposed. This retreat can take place after six to twelve weeks into the group meetings and should clearly be announced as a training and preparation event for the commitment of becoming a youth peer minister.

One of the first discoveries will be the level of commitment each potential peer minister is willing to make. The retreat must be a requirement for those who want to be peer ministers. It is possible to do some bending as to how much of the retreat is required, but every one of the peer ministers must attend. Here is where the youth ministry director becomes single-minded and, if necessary, authoritarian. For the most part, the youth ministry director must be a model of peer ministry, which is mutual and vulnerable relational ministry. However, an effective peer ministry program must be founded on a clear understanding of commitment. Do not allow peer ministers to be active who do not attend the peer ministry retreats. The peer ministry retreat will separate those who want to be committed to being a peer minister from those who like the idea but cannot find the energy or the time. There will be tons of good excuses, but take the commitment to the peer ministry retreat as non-negotiable because it is foundational. Simply state that "If you cannot make the peer ministry retreat, then you must be inactive as our church's peer minister until another peer ministry retreat is scheduled."

The content of a peer ministry retreat is not simply knowledge or skills, rather the primary purpose is to develop unity, compassion, and caring for one another. It is essential to realize that peer ministry is not as much a skill to be shared, as it is a love and faith to be shared. Peer ministers who share their skills without the support of the other peer ministers will soon become drained and empty. Love and faith are necessarily two-way streets; they are elements of a mutual relationship. To initiate those mutual relationships is often very draining for a period of time. If the peer ministers do not have a supportive group of peers in ministry, the ministry can lose momentum before it gets started. Someone who does not attend the peer ministry retreat could make up the skills and knowledge that are shared, but the warmth and unity that is experienced cannot be made up.

What takes place at the youth peer ministry retreat? There are three major areas to be addressed:

(1) Time to pray. For one another, for spiritual depth and commitment. Time to learn how to pray.
(2) Time to learn skills and practice those skills to one another.
(3) Time to worship as personally and intimately as possible.

Prayer is the primary tool of youth peer ministry because prayer opens the spirit and the heart. We are not speaking of simply listening to prayers or reading prayers. We are speaking of prayer as a yearning of hearts, of love expressed to God and others, of troubles shared in community. The youth peer ministers must be encouraged and taught to pray.

Prayer under these circumstances will be a more directed experience than the prayers in the introductory Bible study and discussion group. Here, encourage a more intimate sharing of doubts, weaknesses, fears, and troubles. For example, you may simply say that you want us all to be thinking of an area of our life that is most troublesome and hurting. Then, ask for the group to sit in a circle and share that trouble or hurt. Then, ask that each one in the circle pray for the hurt or trouble expressed by the person sitting on their right. This allows everyone to be as open as they would dare to be about their troubles and hurts. It emphasizes the importance of listening. It gives some very meaningful practice in prayer.

Another example of more directed, more intimate prayer is to focus on a single peer minister each session. Whatever skill is being taught, that chosen peer minister will be a living experiment. When the session is over, have the group each lay their hands on "the chosen" for that session, each saying a single prayer of encouragement and blessing.

Worship is also a good time to encourage prayer. Having everyone pray a prayer of thanksgiving, a prayer of confession, or a prayer of intercession is very meaningful and often personal. A worship mood can be established by having those asked to pray to hold a candle and pass the candle to the next person who is to pray.

Prayer is a powerful tool in promoting intimacy, love, and faith. A discussion may remain distant and objective, learning may be clear and wise, but without personal application then, suddenly, prayer brings tears, emotion, intimacy, and warmth— where hours of teaching and discussion failed to even crack the surface.

The peer ministry retreat must also be the place to learn the skills of peer ministry, but more important those skills must be practiced. Listening skills are taught, but more important, the peer ministers listen to one another. Ways of identifying youth at risk or in crisis are discussed, but more important, the peer ministers share their crises, their doubts, their weaknesses with one another.

The peer ministry retreat is a time of worship. Here, give the peer ministers an opportunity to interpret scripture on their own and to share their interpretations with one another. Confess failures and weaknesses to one another. Use popular music to stimulate worship as a call to reach out to the world. Play contemporary Christian music that speaks the themes of the retreat. Be creative. Be intimate. Share tears. Share troubles. Share love and encouragement.

The final task of the retreat is to consider a "letter of commitment" for everyone who attends. The letter of commitment should be introduced and considered, but not yet signed. It is best to interview individually each peer minister candidate before signing the commitment. At the interview, speak to the youth peer minister about the kinds of commitments that are required and the kinds of commitments that are optional. Optional commitments are areas of ministry where peer ministers may use their skills and caring to benefit the youth ministries of the church. Usually this would mean such ministries as being a counselor for youth events, trips, or retreats. A sampling of those ministries could be confirmation retreats or camps, work camps, choir tours, vacation Bible school, day camps for children, and such.

Advise the youth peer ministers never to discipline. That is not a role of the youth peer minister, and it is difficult at best for one youth to discipline another. In a peer ministry setting, there is a wonderful cooperation rather than a sense of being watched, and so youth do not spend time planning what they can "get away with." When discipline is necessary, the youth ministry director, lay leader, or pastor should be responsible. Even "discipline" can be done with a listening attitude rather than a condemning one or a correctional one. Pull the problem youth out of the group and form a small group of the less cooperative youth. This group often turns out to be youth at risk with difficult problems at home or in school.

The planning for the first retreat or camp at which the youth peer ministers can apply their skills is both exciting and crucial. A retreat is probably preferable if you do not have confirmation retreats or camps as a part of your church's history. On the other hand, camp may take more preparation or energy, but is often more rewarding. Do not go to a camp where the counselors are provided, unless the camp is open to having your peer ministers counsel with the resident counselors. The best thing that can happen at confirmation camp is the relationship that forms between the counselor and the camper. If only resident camp counselors are at the camp you attend, then the benefits of those relationships will stay at the camp. If you bring your own peer counselors, then the benefit of the counselor-camper relationship can be taken home with you and will enrich your ministry programs.

The following is a typical daily schedule for a retreat or camp.

8:00 A.M.   Wake-up

8:45 A.M.   Assemble in the dining hall prior to breakfast.
                (1) make announcements
                (2) do something fun: tell a funny story, ask for a volunteer and give them an amusing task or assignment
                (3) explain the schedule for the day and pray

9:00 A.M.   Breakfast

9:30 A.M.   Session #1
                (1) sing
                (2) have peer ministers introduce the theme using personal examples and testimony
                (3) divide into small groups led by the peer ministers for discussion and prayer
                (4) return to the large group for reporting of discussions and closing songs

10:45 A.M.   15-minute break

11:00 A.M.   Session #2 (following same outline for #1)

12:30 P.M.   Lunch

1:00-4:00 P.M. Free time (Encourage the youth peer ministers to spend at least fifteen minutes with each of the youth in their small group on a one-to-one basis during the "free time" opportunities.)

4:00 P.M.   Session #3
                (1) meet to sing and pray
                (2) assign each group the task of developing a skit or a visual presentation to go with the playing

| | of a song by a modern or contemporary Christian musician to be performed at the evening worship |

6:00 P.M.   Dinner
7:00 P.M.   Session #4 (following the same outline for
              #1 and #2)
8:15 P.M.   15-minute break
8:30 P.M.   Session #5
              (1) meet to sing and pray
              (2) work on skits or music visuals to be performed
              at the evening worship
10:30 P.M.   Evening worship
              (1) sing
              (2) try creative prayer or confession
              (3) have each group perform; stress the desire
              to have a scripture passage to read along with
              the skit or visual
              (4) if possible, share communion
              (5) close in darkness with a lone candle and
              free prayers
11:30 P.M.   In-cabin devotions

The key to a successful retreat or camp is training the youth peer ministers to resist natural tendencies to group together as important leaders and shut out the participants of the camp or retreat. On the ride to the retreat or camp, require each of the peer ministers to learn the names of each participant. Do not just introduce yourself and forget, but mentally practice and learn everyone's name. Call out names whenever possible. Address everyone by name in learning sessions, at meals, in games—all the time. Ask peer ministers to walk up and down the bus aisle until they know everyone's name. The tendency, especially of adults, is to sit in front of the bus and never even attempt to interact with the youth. The same general rule should be noted at meals. Trained peer ministers must interact with the youth at meals and again resist the natural tendency to eat separately as selected representatives of the group. This is much more difficult than it sounds. To understand how difficult, any adult ordained minister knows how much rethinking must take place to become a peer and a servant in the congregation. More so than any other kind of ministry, it is vital that meaningful interaction with the youth takes place in informal settings. The rule of thumb is that when you are a peer minister, you are a peer minister all the time—not just when leading a small group, not just in learning sessions, not just in worship, but all the time. Instruct the peer ministers to make themselves vulnerable by being willing to stand alone. A peer minister alone is vulnerable and approachable. A peer minister in a group of two is twice as hard to approach, in a group of three is three times as hard to approach, and in a group of four is impossible to approach as a peer.

One of the most effective tools of the peer minister at a retreat or camp is the evening devotion in cabin groups. Each peer minister, or perhaps a pair of peer ministers, is assigned a cabin group of the same sex. Just before going to bed, gather the entire cabin or dorm group for devotions. The devotion should have three elements: (1) a scripture or other reading lesson, (2) a time for significant personal self-disclosure that everyone partici-pates in, and (3) prayer.

The setting must be conducive to intimacy. Do not allow the youth to stay in their beds. Let them take their pillows and blankets and form a circle in the middle of the room. They may be tired, but don't let them sleep yet. Another general rule is that the group will take on the characteristics of a living entity, and if just one partici-pant fails to participate for any reason, be it falling asleep or other, the life of the group will be drained and the ability of each member to participate severely lessened. Once everyone is comfortable and together, the mood and the focus of the group can be assisted by turning off all the lights and placing a lit candle in the center of the circle. Then the mood can best be set by a Bible story or a story from another source of literature. It is very important that the peer minister lead by example. When asking a personal question, the peer minister should be the first to answer that question. Be as open and as honest as possible. Even be painfully honest if in sincerity that is who you are and an accurate testimony to your life. Leadership in a peer ministry sense is not to get out in front and give orders, but rather, to get behind, lead by example, and be an example of humility, brokenness, and weakness. Along these lines, do not be afraid to express doubt. Doubt can be a necessary first step to greater faith. He who does not doubt, does not grow, but he who expresses doubt is searching and longing to grow in faith.

Adolescence is often a time of spiritual crisis that can elicit a great deal of emotion. What a child often blindly accepts in terms of spiritual faith, an adolescent will question and doubt because of these changes in understanding. Peer ministry encourages the expression of those doubts, but often that expression of doubt is difficult and emotional. Without the expression of doubt, the adolescent will simply grow cold to faith and drift away. If spiritual doubt is allowed expression, there can be a wonderful growth in faith that often is accompanied by tears. A common crisis in faith that most adolescents go through is a deep questioning and doubting of the existence of God. Without an arena to express this doubt, such as that offered in a peer ministry setting, the doubt can kill and destroy faith. On the other hand, where doubt is allowed expression, the same doubt can become the motivation to seek a deeper, more mature understanding of faith. If the adolescent doubts God's love then adolescent behavior may likewise be affected, and often this means an experimentation in very godless values, such as drug and alcohol experimentation, cheating, stealing, and sexual promiscuity. One youth was into all kinds of bad habits because, as he put it, he simply did not think that there was a God who cared. At a time of prayer at camp, the youth expressed his sorrow over his rebellious actions toward God. Later that night, the boy cried for almost an hour, and at one time, went to the outdoor cross, kneeling before it and hugging it. The boy recounted the experience to the youth director and said it was like God was right there when he was crying and he felt so cleansed, so new.

Following a retreat or camp is the ideal time to invite the participants to attend the weekly junior and senior high Bible study. Explain that if they want to keep their newfound relationships going, they can do so by having the same leader they had at the retreat or camp at the weekly Bible study. Following the above-mentioned camp, our junior and senior high Bible study more than doubled in size. With peer ministry, the gains made in relationships and spiritual depth can be continued throughout the year.

The additional participation in the junior and senior high Bible study group will gradually decline. Do not be worried! The attendance at the weekly Bible study will increase after each retreat or camp and in the fall when school starts. Attendance will decline the longer it has been since the last retreat or camp, and in the spring. It is impossible to completely recreate in the weekly groups the positive effects of small groups at the retreats or camps. There is something about the cumulative effect of eating together, sleeping together, playing together, worshiping together that cannot be completely recreated at a weekly meeting. But the positive effects will last longer and for more youth retreat after retreat, camp after camp. The second retreat will be better than the first, and the third will be better than the second, "better" meaning that the youth will expect and get more out of it, they will become more intimately self-disclosing and move to self-disclosure more quickly. They will become progressively more serious, more mature, more caring, more loving, more spiritually in tune, more creative, and more constructive. There is a tendency, as the weekly Bible study dwindles, to think it was just a flash in the pan, a fleeting experience. It is not true. The success of the retreats year after year will depend on previous retreats. There is a cumulative effect. As a whole, over time, as a group, spiritual depth is developed and becomes more permanent.

This second year, it is good to begin a "CIT" or "Counselor-in-Training" program. Invite juniors and seniors in high school to be youth peer ministers. Usually the youth peer ministers will act as counselors for all junior and senior high events, but primarily they will act as counselors for the confirmation retreat and camp each year. Confirmation instruction is typically for seventh to ninth graders. That leaves tenth graders too old to attend confirmation retreats and camps and too young to be youth peer ministers. Put them into a CIT program designed specifically for the tenth grade. Those tenth graders involved in Bible study are asked if they would like to train to become youth peer ministers. If they have gone to camps or retreats often, that is exactly what they dream of. Most who are positively influenced by a youth peer minister want to become youth peer ministers. At a summer camp, announce the CIT program and how participation is dependent upon their faithfulness to weekly Bible study. The CITs are invited to attend the late fall or winter Peer Ministry Training event. They will be paired with peer ministry counselors at the Confirmation retreat or camp. The CITs will then go to the late summer Peer Ministry Training event and be able to make a commitment to becoming Peer Ministers in time for the fall program. This "farm system" provides a good transition from being in confirmation to becoming youth peer ministers.

During the second year, start what we have called an HIP retreat, or Helping Is Personal. This retreat is for those youth who are in junior or senior high who want to be in a teenage support group. They are teens at risk, teens from broken homes, teens with self-destructive tendencies or other problems. The only criteria for coming to the HIP retreat is a serious problem and a willingness to share with others having similar problems. Try to make this a cost-free retreat. Often it will take place at the church or at a home. The church pays for the food. The retreat runs from Friday evening to Saturday lunch. The youth bring sleeping bags and pillows and sleep on the floor. Wait for the second year to begin this type of retreat because the youth need to have developed a certain level of trust with the youth director, lay leader or pastor, and the youth peer ministers. The format for the retreat is four to five sessions where a topic is introduced and then discussed with a youth peer minister leading. The group size should be three to four youth. Depth in discussion is a must. The topics often center on parents, self-image, depression, fear, pressures of life, and such. Again, prayer is an important element.

It is also very important to recognize and affirm the youth peer ministers in their ministry efforts. This can be done in many ways, but here are a few ways that have been found effective. Try writing personal letters to the youth peer ministers after an event where they have acted as counselors. Verbal thanks and praise is inspiring for the moment and also effective, but a written note gives them a tangible gift they can refer to and keep. Try to have T-shirts printed with a youth peer ministry logo to affirm their identity. Have one of the youth come up with the design. Have them all vote on a color. Try to pay the way of the youth peer ministers to be counselors at a confirmation retreat or camp and give a significant discount to senior high trips or events. A meal together to celebrate a birthday or the accomplishment of an event can be fun and affirming. Remember their birthday and celebrate their important events.

Many secondary ministries will spring from a youth peer ministry program. Youth are ministers, so do everything possible to give them ministry opportunities. Think of their talents and seemingly endless energy and enthusiasm. Musical talents? How about a touring choir, orchestra, drama group, puppeteers, and so on. Harness the talents, focus the talents on a ministry objective and stand back in awe at the quality and dedication these youth will show toward their Lord. If there is a tour during the summer or a vacation break, have daily Bible study and devotions in small groups, so the youth peer ministers can have their skills utilized in leading these groups. From these small groups, give the peer ministers individual responsibility. Have group leaders pray daily for the youth of their small group and have them spend at least fifteen minutes of one-on-one time with the members of their small groups at some time during the trip. When counting heads, don't count all the individual heads, rather count the peer minister heads and have each counselor account for the whereabouts of the members of their group.

Youth are very idealistic. Attack poverty with your youth. What about a work camp or servant project? Again, allow youth peer ministers to help lead the work groups. They could also be responsible for a devotion to start the day and prayer to end the day. Work camps and servant projects should also be discussed to have their full positive impact felt. Allow peer ministers to lead those discussions.

Youth peer ministers make excellent helpers in vacation Bible school or Sunday school but it is *not* good to use them as classroom teachers. Though new techniques for facilitation and team teaching are redifining education as a partnership, a classroom teacher is often perceived in a more hierarchical role, and it may be difficult and too much to ask of a peer minister. The same may be said of confirmation instruction. Encourage peer ministers to lead discussions on the topic, but not to lead the class from a position of authority.

Youth peer ministry is a powerful and exciting form of ministry that can create a youth ministry that will perpetuate itself. Youth peer ministry fosters youth as ministers, and no one can minister to the heart, mind, and spirit of a youth like another youth.

Ted Stump, director of Touch Phoenix Ministries, in Phoenix, Arizona, has developed a wonderful outreach program to bring the gospel to the youth community. Ted describes the ministry as a "cell group-based youth ministry." It is, in fact, cell group-based youth *peer* ministry. The cell groups are described as "discussion groups which meet during the week in students' homes under the leadership of students who desire to minister to their friends. The small group atmosphere is one of love, caring, and acceptance in which the gospel can be made relevant in the lives of our youth."

Ted's approach to youth evangelism is centered in Peer Ministry, in which teens minister to teens. Ted's manual states that the first step is "People First, Program Second." Youth are recruited and trained as ministers who must be teachable and willing to commit themselves to the time and energy demands of the ministry.

The second step is to share the vision with those recruited. Ted explains that the two fundamental questions to be asked of the prospective youth ministers are: "Are you convinced?" and "Can you convince others?" Many different talents will be enlisted, but if the motivation to share the vision is wrong, the ministry will go nowhere.

The third step is to train the youth ministers as servant leaders. The motivation to minister to youth is not to gain a following that will respect and honor the leader. Rather, servant leadership is a humble leadership where the motivation is to give without recognition or reward for the benefit of others.

The fourth step is to give the youth peer ministers ownership of the ministry. This is not an adult program that uses youth ministers, it is a youth program that is for youth and by youth. Ted explains, "The youth *must* take on the responsibilities to turn their campuses upside down for Christ. It must be the burden and concern of our youth to change the world around them."

Once the people are in place, the program can be revealed and take shape. Ted's ministry to the unchurched youth of the community is based on what he describes as "the home cell group." In Acts 2:42-46, the church that resulted from the thousands of believers that were converted at Pentecost was a small group home ministry. That is exactly the kind of ministry Ted is promoting. Ted describes that small group meeting in the homes of youth, led by the youth, as a cell group. The cell group may consist of as few as three members and as many as fifteen members. The group is asked to split when it stabilizes at fifteen. Each group will have:

(1) A servant leader: who leads the group time of one and a half hours weekly.
(2) A servant intern: who is learning to lead and will lead if the group splits.
(3) Encourager: an adult who is pro-youth, who supports the servant leader and servant intern.

The cell group is not a Bible study. It is a group discussion on the heartfelt needs of the youth who attend. The goal is to establish a network of small cell groups at every junior and senior high school. The cell group format is as follows:

(1) Food and unstructured interaction for fifteen minutes.
(2) Introduction of guests and a game or activity that encourages nonthreatening interaction for ten minutes.

(3) A brief statement of the purpose and the format of the group by the servant intern for five minutes.

(4) Topical discussion on a youth concern such as self-worth, failure and success, anger, dating and sex, cliques for thirty minutes.

(5) Prayer, at first led by group leaders, but where the entire cell is eventually asked to pray out loud about concerns expressed by themselves and others.

Ted explains that each cell group's leadership is seeking youth from three areas for participation:

(1) Nonbelievers but seekers.

(2) New believers in need of ministry because of a broken home life or the experience of a close-felt death or an expressed concern or trouble.

(3) Believers who are potential leaders.

Ted believes that the best cell groups will have an equal distribution of youth from each of the three areas. Nonbelievers are inspired by new believers who hurt but are able to find comfort and answers to tough questions. New believers risk self-disclosure of their intimate problems and troubles by the gentle nurturing of believers whose servant leadership does not give advice, but does give a shoulder to cry on, a heart to be moved, and a faith that inspires. One part of the group ministers to the other through shared concerns, opinions, and troubles.

Ted also has a broader vision for this ministry within the home cell group. The leadership of the cell group: a servant leader, a servant intern, and the encourager, need also to be led. Leadership that is not trained and led by a more mature leader is leadership that will eventually wither on the vine. One cannot drink from an empty cup and cell group leaders need opportunities to be filled. Ted proposes the role of a "zone servant." The zone servant is an adult who is a trained minister with youth ministry experiences. The zone servant may be a pastor. The zone servant must be mature and have a love for youth ministry.

The responsibilities of the zone servants are as follows:

(1) To seek to understand the vision of the senior pastor of the sponsoring church and/or the director of youth ministries, and be dedicated to carrying out that vision.

(2) To maintain weekly contact with each school's servant leaders.

(3) To meet weekly with the sponsoring church's pastor and/or Youth ministry director.

(4) To attend as many special youth activities in the zone as possible, such as games, plays, graduations, and special events.

(5) To be available for counseling for those who are ministered to in their zone who have special needs.

(6) To work on developing servant leaders through training.

(7) To make sure that each cell group in their zone is properly conducted.

(8) To attend zone servant meetings and visit cells in their zone as time permits.

The zone servant in Ted's design should be responsible for no more than five servant leaders. If there are more servant leaders in the community, then more zone servants need to be recruited. If there are more than five zone servants taking care of five servant leaders each, then another position, that of a "zone pastor," should be recruited to lead the zone servants. Peers minister to peers in effective ways; all peers in ministry need the support and caring of a peer leader who is there for the specific purpose of caring for the spiritual development of that leader. Ted's youth ministry vision does that while centering the ministry where our youth are: in the schools and in their homes.

Youth Encounter is a national youth organization that, for over thirty years, has organized youth events and practiced youth peer ministry with a college-aged team ministry that leads these events with music and drama. Recently, Youth Encounter pioneered a new model for these events called a "summit" that offers a youth leadership training event for junior and senior high youth. This leadership training event focuses on four areas:

(1) Youth peer ministry training
(2) Youth evangelism training following Ted Stump's model
(3) Youth servant projects
(4) Models of ministry to implement the above in their particular ministry setting

A summit is the perfect place to introduce your church to the youth ministry outlined here. Contact Youth Encounter, 2500 39th Avenue N.E., Minneapolis, Minnestoa 55421. The youth summit and other youth events have locations all over the country and your youth will be inspired by their participation.

Youth ministry can lead a church to revival. Youth are open to change and they enjoy taking risks. Gone are the days when the youth culture will simply fall in line with the faith of their parents. In many instances, the parents have fallen away from the church because these parents, as youth, were ineffectively evangelized. If your church can learn to appeal to you, they will find that these years hold the greatest opportunity in the life of an individual to make significant spiritual changes. Once "set in their ways," spiritual change will come with far greater difficulty, and often only a crisis will provide an opportunity for evangelism. The church of the twenty-first century will be a church that does youth ministry well. A church that does not do youth ministry well will eventually suffer devastating consequences. One of the best ways today to reach the unchurched is to reach their youth. If youth and children can be effectively ministered to in the church, the family can be restored via that ministry.

3

FAMILY MINISTRY
THAT REACHES OUT

The problem with most small group ministries of the church is that they become exclusive and fail to truly welcome the stranger or the visitor. Small group ministry has traditionally been the exclusive domain of a church's women's organization. These women's organizations are increasingly becoming a haven for older women and, as they die, this form of ministry is dying with them. With more and more women pursuing employment, there is less opportunity for women to join these groups and, more importantly, there is less need. The traditional need being met by women's organizations, often called "circles," is fellowship and support. Often, modern working women find those needs met from within their employment contacts. Unfortunately, fewer women are finding the fellowship and support they need within their families.

The same may be said of men. Men traditionally have not met their fellowship and support needs through the church. Men have met and continue to meet those needs through their personal contacts at their places of employment or recreation. Like the modern woman, the modern man is looking for meaningful relationships with those they work or play with. But men are becoming alienated from their families. At one time, the children and the wife were an integral part of an agrarian or even a small business society. Families bonded together because they worked together on the family farm or in the family business. Now farming is big corporate business, and, though small businesses are responsible for the growth in jobs, small businesses fail at a rapid pace, or larger businesses gobble them up, if they are successful. With this kind of discontinuity in the workplace—and the workplace is responsible as much as other beseiged institutions in our society—the family is disintegrating as each members goes their separate ways, as ships passing in the night.

Proof that men are seeking intimacy in their marriages and families is the success of the small group-supported and conference-inspired ministry called "Promise Keepers." Here is a nondenominational ministry for men designed to bring them into an intimate relationship with their wives and children that has influenced thousands of men across the nation.

If the church is going to fill a great need in our society, it can do so by being the catalyst that brings the family together again. Many fathers and mothers who spend little time with their families because of social and cultural circumstances are looking for ways to come together as a family. Frankly, the church has added to the disintegration of the family by separating each member of the family into their own learning and, in some cases, their own worship experience. Some congregations have simultaneous adult worship and Sunday school, which means parents never study, children never worship, and parents and children are driven apart. We have Sunday school and adult Sunday school, but we never think of having a family school where children and adults come together to learn about their faith. Nor do we consider a family worship where parents and children are encouraged to worship together, having portions of the service adult specific, other parts children specific, and some parts cross-generational. Family-centered education, where families use learning stations or directed interactions, is a fruitful ministry possibility for the church of the future.

The family, however, is not simply in need of time together. The family needs to develop intimacy together. Intimacy is more a product of sharing fears, weaknesses, and doubts, rather than the sharing of strengths, wisdom, and accomplishments. The community and the schools will bring families together to share strengths and accomplishments, especially via sports, the arts, and academics. But who will help families share their fears, weaknesses, and doubts, which provides the opportunity for even greater intimacy? For the family to be strengthened, family members must learn from each other and be given the tools to minister to each other. A time of the heart is needed in family life today, and what better institution for the family to look to in providing tools for intimacy, skills for intimacy, and the learning required for intimacy than the church?

Some family members may not see the need for intimacy because they have found that intimacy in other places. Family life that provides intimacy will, in turn, provide motivation for more and deeper forms of interaction and intimacy. If intimacy within the family can be given root, it will grow by the powers that initial root provides. Provide intimacy for relationships from within the family, and the relationships will become motivating and self-perpetuating.

The first step in promoting intimacy from within the family relationships is to take away the demands we place on each other within our modern families. Intimacy is based on the sharing of intimate feelings, in particular, the painful feelings of weakness, fear, and doubts. However, today we tend to share powers, strengths, and talents because we live in a competitive society. Competition in itself is not bad, certainly the children's ministry proposed in chapter 1 has elements of competition. But competition by itself is unfulfilling and incapable of meeting deeper needs. Children are compelled to succeed in school, sports, and the arts. Husbands seek the competition of upward mobility. Wives often are socially competitive, and now more frequently seek recognition in the job market. We all push, achieve, succeed, buy more, and live less. The family has fallen prey to members who share powers, strengths, and talents but that leave its members emotionally desolate and barren. To fill the family with compassion and sensitivity, each family member must be given the tools and opportunities to share intimate feelings, especially those feelings that are centered in the weaker side of our character. Competition is the way of the world we live in, but the church must offer more.

The modern family is looking for intimacy, but they have few or no skills to offer one another in making this happen. The family needs to learn intergenerational ministry.[2] Intergenerational ministry is not as much another program, but rather providing opportunities for adults to spend quality time with children. Quality time is interaction between adults and children that is as close to one-on-one as possible. Children today are craving adult interaction. What is needed is not as much the sharing of a task, but the building of a relationship. Face-to-face interaction is so rare between adults and children, but it is desperately needed. Intergenerational ministry is ministry that is mutual, in that family members seek to learn from one another and discover faith and love together. A ministry of the family that emphasizes the sharing of fears, weaknesses, and doubts, rather than the pressure to succeed through the sharing of strengths, powers, and talents. Such ministries were attempted in the 1960s and 1970s, but they were driven by the church leadership, or they had a programmatic motivation. To succeed in our over-scheduled society, intergenerational learning must be initiated from within the family.

The parent is still the natural leader of the family. The parent has what children need. Children need values and standards that they cannot discover on their own. Parents need to correct and discipline children who often seek their own self-interest at the expense of their own safety and welfare. However, parents also need to learn the value of play and creativity that the children of the family would gladly teach them. Families need to rediscover the positive contributions of stability and wisdom that the grandparents can offer. The family needs to come together again to share the perspectives of each generation in their wisdom and value. Families need to rediscover their hearts as the most important source of intimacy in communication. The church can provide the tools and the experience to facilitate this new direction of intergenerational ministry within the family.

Before the generations represented in the family seek to give and receive from the generations around them in the family, the family members must gain an appreciation for what these generations have to offer. There is nothing more difficult than to convince a teen that their parents' wisdom, direction, and discipline are something they should value and not resent. It is difficult for parents to even imagine learning from their children about how to play as a constructive use of time. It makes little sense to repeat mistakes made in the past, but without an appreciation of the wisdom of the older generation and their wealth of experiences, the value of the older generation will largely remain untapped. Families must begin with the appreciation of each family member, regardless of age, as a child of God with a wealth of love and faith that only they can offer.

The next step is for each family member to make themselves vulnerable to each other. Not only to respect one another, but also to share one another's burdens. Through an attitude of mutual ministry, family members can learn to share weaknesses, fears, and faults in a safe and affirming, even forgiving, environment. Once family members take the risk of becoming vulnerable to each other, then they will be motivated to learn from each other without resentment or distrust.

The generation of power within the family is the middle generation, or the parent. For intergenerational ministry to take place, the parent of the family must be committed to its implementation. The youth leader knows that it is important to create peer learning opportunities within the youth culture, and independent of their parents. Youth have little power to make changes within the family. Parents will not naturally learn from their youth, so they must be taught to learn from their children, and they must be willing to be taught. If parents can be taught the importance of intergenerational ministry within the family, then parents will have the power to implement that ministry. However, there is an attitude within our society that is working against that power. In our modern society, many parents have given up their leadership role to "professionals" with the mistaken assumption that parenting is a definable role that can best be farmed out to others. Parents leave spiritual values for church professionals to teach. Education is left for school professionals. Physical fitness is left for sports teams to teach. Entertainment is left to the TV computer, or the play toy to teach. In large measure, parents have given up too much. Parents are finding themselves at a distance and alienated from their children. There is no better place to reverse this trend than in our churches.

To teach parents the power they have to implement an intergenerational family ministry and to give parents the education, tools, and models to make that happen, try forming a parenting class. Young parents are often eager to get their families off to a good start, but this is important for parents with all ages of children. It is never too late. Parents with younger children need to learn to play, parents with older children need to learn to be vulnerable and to seek to receive from their children, as well as give. This is so important, so try taking the content outline and the topics for the parenting class and publishing them in the church newsletter. Even those who do not attend can at least get a taste of what is needed to begin an intergenerational ministry within their family. Here is a possible parenting class outline:

Part One—Parenting Authority

Session 1. Rules are values, which are tangibly implemented. Determine rules that are "no compromise" rules. These rules must be enforced at all cost. Determine behavior that should not be enforced with rules. These behaviors are reinforced with rewards and praise.

Session 2. Bring out self-affirming independence from children. What children have to offer the family. The art of play. The art of the family discussion. Family spirituality through scripture study and prayer.

Session 3. Understand the importance of grandparents. Discover how parenting is influenced by how the parent was parented. The role of a grandparent who is either dead or separated by great distances from the family. The death of a grandparent is often the single biggest crisis in a youth or child's life.

Part Two—Parenting As Your Child's Best Friend

Session 1. The art of mutual family ministry. How can we learn from our children as much as we hope to teach? How can we, as parents, learn from our parents and incorporate the grandparents' wisdom into the family?

Session 2. The art of sharing weaknesses. The art of sharing faults. The art of sharing fears. The art of sharing doubts.

Session 3. Practical helps for bringing the family together. The day off dedicated to the family. Family worship. Family vacations that are dedicated to friendship and love rather than activities and travel that can push the family apart.

This outline is all anyone needs to start their own parenting class. The class will be most effective if it is a discussion. Do not seek to give answers, seek to discover answers from the participants who attend.

Another model for intergenerational parenting ministry is what we have previously on page 31 called "Intergenerational Bible Studies." These study groups meet in homes and are open to anyone in the congregation. Families with children, families without children, families with infants, families with children grown and independent, singles, widows—anyone is invited to come. Here the "family" is more accurately a church family, but it is in fact a "family" with all the diversity of ages and interests.

The power of the intergenerational Bible study is that anyone in the congregation can participate in this "family" group and everyone can learn from one another. The lonely can be included in a personal and inviting way. The singles can be a part of a family that many long for but have no avenue in which to participate. This kind of group would be especially attractive to new members because everyone starts out as strangers and there are no criteria to meet for membership.

Family ministry is one of the best ways to invite the community. First, everyone wants to improve their family relationships, and parents want to improve their parenting skills. Second, these ministries meet in homes, and that is often a more neutral ground than the church building. If the group is going to be inviting to the community, it must be the responsibility of every member of the group to invite someone who may be interested. Further, it is the responsibility of the group's leadership to continue to encourage those invitations. When advertising a group, always conclude the article with: "Friends are always welcome to join us."

The intergenerational groups are led by trained lay leaders and lay leaders have the strongest witness in the community. It's been said that if you are going to buy a car, would you be more likely to take the advice of a paid salesperson or a satisfied customer. The satisfied customer wins every time. Lay leaders are satisfied customers. Clergy are paid salespeople in the eyes of the community.

4

SOCIAL MINISTRY
THAT REACHES OUT

Social ministry is evangelism through the intimacy of social interactions. This is not the social interaction of the visitor trying to break into an established social group within the church at predictable "fellowship" opportunities. This is rather the church reaching out to its community and trying to incarnate the gospel where the community gathers. This is a risky and difficult switch. It is very difficult for us as a church to be the new voice of Christ to an established community group. Yet do we not ask of our visitors the same risks and difficult task? Do we not ask our visitors to somehow break into our church's established groups with their own power and resources? Would it not be more reasonable, and faithful for the church to meet the community where it is, where the community feels comfortable and nonthreatened, so that the gospel can be communicated effectively? We, in effect, ask visitors to evangelize themselves, using their own initiative and their own powers. We need to mobilize the people of God to do the work of Christ. We need to be taking the risks in initiating the contact by using our resources and powers. Here are several practical examples of how to accomplish that.

To have an effective evangelism program, two avenues may be traveled. Either meet the social and spiritual needs of the people being sought as members, or recruit the community to join forces with the church to meet the needs of others. Ted Stump's high school-centered youth ministry, and the description of a new family ministry that helps families rediscover intimacy between generations, each offer ways to meet the needs of those within the group. There are, other exciting ways to recruit the community to join the church in meeting the needs of others.

Many churches describe this as social ministry and, for many churches, it is the dormant committee of the church. Often, social ministry means nothing more than a yearly food drive for the local food shelf. If more is done, it is usually done by a small and drained group of volunteers who never change. Usually other efforts occur periodically to raise money for a noble cause, but it is much more rare to find a congregation that actually tackles, with the resources of money, people, and space, a more challenging venture.

Often, a church will hesitate because of a lack of volunteers. Why not advertise for those volunteers in the local newspaper? For example, an advertisement could read: "Christ Church is taking on a ministry for the homeless: food donations and meal preparation, finding shelters, education, and training, job search, child care and all that is necessary to restabilize the community a family living on the street. Would you like to help in any way? Call the church at 555-5555 for more information." What a witness to what the church is dedicated to do in ministry and what a wonderful way to invite the community to not only join the church but, better yet, to become active immediately within the church. Social ministry can take on the following dimensions:

(1) Hands-on help programs

(2) Mobilizing the church community to donate money and resources

(3) Political advocacy

(4) International or inner city assistance

(5) Home repair assistance

Hands-On Help Programs

If the church wants to validate its ministry to the community, it is vital that the church support various kinds of hands-on helping ministries on a regular basis. Where its poor and helpless are offered assistance, Jesus is revealed in the face of those poor and helpless. It is, in fact, a deeply spiritual undertaking. Any growing church must cover this base with care. Further, do not simply do the work, but make sure that the work is reported and celebrated. Install the lay ministers who participate. Publish the accomplishments in detail. Give time during the worship for volunteers to report their experiences. Preach it. Teach it. This ministry is not merely a collection ministry where resources are given to an organization that does the work. That is something altogether different. Do the work! The ministry being proposed is where the church members who volunteer to feed the poor actually feed the poor with face-to-face, long-term interaction that includes education opportunities and may lead to worshiping together. A tutoring program for neighborhood children also provides an opportunity for a face-to-face ministry that may be a good place to start because there is less fear associated with children as opposed to the poor. Fear may be the biggest liability in initiating face-to-face ministry.

Press Release: Christ Church invites you to join us in the church parking lot at 6:00 P.M. each Wednesday evening to travel to the inner city food and clothing distribution center. Help us to help the less fortunate.

or

Press release: Our neighborhood elementary school is in need of tutors for children who need help with their homework and an adult friend. Join Christ Church in offering two 45-minute tutoring sessions from 3:00-4:00 P.M. two or four days each week. Invest yourself one on one with the children of our neighborhood.

Mobilizing the Church Community to Donate Money and Resources

This work is what most churches define as social ministry and it is probably the least rewarding of the five social ministry areas outlined. The problem is that on the one end, it is an organizational effort that can be tedious and time consuming and on the other end, those who donate their money and resources rarely see and experience the ministry they are supporting at work. This is an essential phase of social ministry, but it does little to inspire and reap the fruits of social ministry. It can be done creatively. Give out grocery bags with a shopping list the Sunday before a food drive. Put crosses on a Christmas tree that give a name and a specific request by a shut-in for a Christmas gift. Adopt a family in need and introduce the family to the congregation.

For publication in the church newsletter: "For Lent we ask each of you to consider putting aside $1.00 each day to support the New Life Center for battered women and children. We have two families from our congregation who have used this facility at their time of greatest need. 'Let us bear one another's burdens and so fulfill the law of Christ.' "

Political Advocacy

Many churches are being asked to unite with other Judeo-Christian churches and synagogues to make a political statement to the local authorities and influence public funds for social programs supported by the religious community. These organizations are making a powerful impact on our communities, and churches that fail to join the effort will appear self-serving and uncaring. Parochialism can only hurt the church. Be a team player or risk the label of arrogance and insensitivity that will certainly hurt the evangelism efforts of the church.

Press release: The following churches have united with our county government to offer a youth jobs program. Each of the listed churches will provide a youth mentor to not only provide a job, but also provide a friend and adult counsel.

International or Inner City Assistance

Do not let your own community's boundaries limit your social ministry efforts. Missionary support is one thing, but it is quite another to send your own ministers into foreign or domestic ministry settings. We have always sent youth and adults to work camps to help repair the homes of the poor. We have gone to the poor of the Appalachian Mountains through the Appalachian Service Project (ASP), to an inner city work camp in Minneapolis in the Phillips Neighborhood sponsored by Lutheran Social Service of Minnesota, or to a home building project in Aqua Prieta, Mexico across from Douglas, Arizona. We recruit sponsors for our youth who pay the way of our youth to attend while the youth, in turn, write reports and letters of thanks to share the ministry with their sponsors. The experiences can be life-changing. Youth and adults who may be interested in nothing else in the church will latch on to this ministry and make it a yearly commitment. It is ministry that is exciting and that makes a tangible difference. Usually these ministries require a weekend or weeklong time commitment. Usually the workers get to know the people who are helped intimately. The love flows with a power that is beautiful to see.

Work camps provide one expression of service. Another is running a vacation Bible school for a remote ministry setting. We have been involved with a vacation Bible school for the Cree Native Americans in remote villages in Canada through LAMP (Lutheran Association of Missionaries and Pilots) and a vacation Bible school for the Navajo Native Americans in Rock Point, Arizona. Again, the rewards of this ministry cannot be duplicated in the local setting. It is cross-cultural, and working with poor children can literally melt your heart away.

> Press Release: Interested in a free trip to Mexico with Christ Church? Wait, there is a catch! Christ Church is building a home for an abandoned mother with four children who are currently living in a home constructed out of cardboard boxes. Would you spend a week in Mexico to help us build a home for this family? Call the church for details.

Home Repair Assistance

I have found that given the right skills and the right attitudes toward sharing talents, any given church has skilled laborers such as carpenters, electricians, and plumbers who would be willing to donate their skills to help the poor. We have a form that people can use to apply for assistance and each application is given a prioritized ranking depending on the intensity of the need and the availability of the right skills to do the job. What a blessing this could be to the community. What a witness to the love of Christ!

> Press Release: Can you afford to hire the necessary help to get the needed repairs done—water damage, dangerous electrical problems, or a plumbing crisis? Christ Church offers volunteer labor to those who apply. You must be able to pay for materials, but Christ Church will supply the labor. Call the church for your application. If you have skills to share with those who need assistance, join us today.

Many churches are abandoning the inner city because of its poverty and crime, in spite of the fact that the inner city is the greatest mission field today. A church that is dedicated to meeting the needs of the poor within the city will be a church that will grow and flourish. It is vital to have a vision for the ministry that can mobilize resources and yet meet desperate needs with Christian love and faithfulness.

One idea that works is to establish a ministry that pairs suburban congregations with churches trying to survive impoverished neighborhoods. To accomplish this, a cooperation between churches must be established. For example, many churches are now involved in a program that feeds the poor or offers clothing. But feeding the poor and clothing them doesn't break the cycle of poverty. Why not have a congregation adopt a poor family and work with that family to break the cycle of poverty and restabilize them back into the community? Work with a poor family by offering job training, counseling, child care, and education. Churches want to make a difference, and this idea really makes a difference. Our country as a whole is getting frustrated with "answers" to social problems that actually sustain and perpetuate problems. This is a real answer that makes a difference.

The key to this ministry is a social service agency that can screen families for the restabilization effort and provide expertise in the complex areas of social service needs that no doubt will be uncovered. This ministry must include education for the assisting churches and a sensitivity to the complexity of poverty issues. The program can be run much like the refugee programs that were done in the past. The refugees are now from our own cities.

Another key issue is housing. Housing that is affordable is in extremely short supply. However, properties are being abandoned in the city because no one is available to maintain them and owners cannot get fair rental values in poverty areas. Why not suggest that property owners donate their building to this ministry effort and then they can take a fair rental value as a tax deduction. Besides the tax benefits, the church could agree to maintain the living spaces and pay a small amount of rent to cover taxes and utilities. Thus, churches are providing housing for little cost and then working with poor families through rent incentives so they can get out of poverty permanently. This is not for all the poor, but for the borderline poor and the working poor. This kind of ministry often turns out to be the push that gets them independent again.

Beyond the social service benefits, there are wonderful ministry possibilities. Many churches provide a children's ministry, such as God's Gifts, for the children of that poor community in the church's housing units. Other churches provide child care, or parenting classes. Once poor families take on flesh and blood, and once the church family is incarnated in those who are not our biological offspring, the ministry areas are endless. People in need are people open to the gospel message. The church that blossoms is a church that takes a proactive stance toward ministry—by reaching new generations of people who were not born in our midst. Jesus said, "Go make disciples," and he did not say, "Sit and wait for the disciples to come to you." Step out and act. You cannot steer a car that's not moving, and God cannot direct your church's ministry unless the church is taking available steps to reach out into the community with the gospel of Jesus Christ.

5

WORSHIP: A GOLDEN KEY OR A RUSTY DOOR?

Perhaps the greatest problem in evangelism by the church is that the church is answering questions no one is asking. This irrelevance cannot be traced to a flaw in the gospel. The good news of Jesus Christ is rich in its application and relevance to our lives. In the church, however, religious style can minimize the gospel message. Many of our churches have a "members only" country-club mentality. There is a pervasive and often not too subtle attitude that the church has what the world needs, and it's not available to outsiders. We stress the "grace of God," but feel that the grace of God is our possession and we are not under obligation to share it. This arrogance is most often a problem of style, not substance. The gospel tells us, even requires us, to share, but we share only from our own perspective, from our own style, and the gospel is hindered, even hidden.

Is there a style of worship where the church can become inviting and not limiting? Is there a style of worship that accepts diversity and does not see unity only within the narrow confines of conformity to a particular worship style? Each church has what is familiar, and the familiar can easily lead to an exclusion of those unfamiliar.

The question is "Does the familiar exclude or invite the unchurched?"

Generally adults appreciate the traditional styles of worship. Most adults are "set in their ways," but not all are! On the other hand, youth tend to appreciate, sometimes even crave, the nontraditional, the creative and the exciting. It is true that once youth find an expression of worship that they enjoy, they may be as uncompromising as their adult counterparts with change, but at least initially, youth seek a new style of worship.

Traditional, formal churches tend to appeal to older generations of believers. Creative and contemporary churches are more likely to appeal to younger generations of believers. The obvious difference is in style and not content. Yet, the first barrier to introducing new styles of worship to traditional churches is to convince the people that new styles of worship do not necessarily affect the content. It may be difficult to convince people, for example, that using guitars to accompany the Lord's Prayer has no different theological implications than having it recited in the familiar place in the worship service with heads bowed.

To make worship appealing to the unchurched, the service must be easy and convenient to learn. A subtle, yet deadly, characteristic of most worship services, regardless of whether they are traditional or contemporary, is a tendency to exclude the visitor. This barrier is the "tyranny of the familiar." The most powerful force that leaves visitors feeling excluded from worship services is the familiar music or liturgy that everyone knows—everyone but the visitor, who is lost. That awkward feeling leaves them to be the last to stand and the last to sit. This oddness causes the visitor to be the only one fumbling for a page in the hymnal, if the visitor happens to have the right hymnal among the options in the pew rack. Familiar hymns or songs are sung with enthusiasm, but the visitor feels separated from the experience, not able to participate with the same enthusiasm. Some of this structure is unavoidable. Certainly the familiar must always be a part of our worship experiences or we too would lose interest in the rituals that open our hearts to God, but we can minimize the negative impact that the familiar can have on the uninitiated.

If worship is to be a golden key that opens the believer's heart to the presence of God, it must fulfill two functions:

(1) Worship must be relevant—"speaks to me."
(2) Worship must be welcoming—"speaks to others."

If worship fails to be relevant and welcoming, worship becomes a rusty door. True, it is a door, but it becomes a barrier to bringing us into God's presence. The door is rusted shut and it might as well be a wall. Rather, worship should be a golden key that opens the door to God's presence. The door is our heart. Worship that is a golden key opens our hearts to the reality of the living God that surrounds us. Golden key worship is first of all relevant.

Worship That Speaks to Me

The story is told of a rabbi's gift. A rabbi visited the abbot of a dying monastery. The rabbi said, "I cannot help you, only mourn with you, but I will say one thing, 'The Messiah is one of you.'" After the rabbi left, everyone in the monastery started to question the rabbi's statement, "The Messiah is one of you." "Who could the rabbi be referring to?" they asked themselves. The obvious choice for the Messiah was the abbot himself. Yes, surely, but the obvious may or may not be correct. Why didn't the rabbi just come out and say the abbot is the Messiah? Perhaps the rabbi was referring to Brother Thomas as the Messiah. He is such a good example of faith, but he does have a bad temper that often gets him into trouble. Maybe the Messiah is Brother Elwood. He's always very energetic, but he does have a thorn in his character, thinking he's always right. How about Brother Philip? He's so peaceful, but almost to the point of being passive. Each member of the monastery considered whether he might be the Messiah. A frightening thought. Each member of the monastery thought that it could be any one of them, and they started treating each other with a renewed sense of respect. They even started treating themselves with respect because, even though the thought was frightening, they couldn't rule out altogether that they were chosen to be the Messiah. The attitude of mutual respect renewed the monastery, saving it. They were never sure who the Messiah was, they were only sure it was one of them.

For worship to be relevant to the worshiper, it must treat each worshiper with respect. Each worshiper in Christ has received the gift of the Holy Spirit. We must learn to respect that Spirit within each of us. Invite the Spirit of God to be expressed by each worshiper, and the cumulative effect will be powerful. "The Messiah is one of you." Actually, in Christ, through the gift of the Holy Spirit, the Messiah dwells within each of us, and only as the Body of Christ in all its appreciation of diversity, can worship take place that is relevant. Worship that is relevant, that "speaks to me," is worship that is:

>   Personal yet communal
>   Emotional yet instructional
>   Inspiring yet practical
>   Spiritual yet tangible

Personal Yet Communal

Too many times worship is so rigidly structured that there is no time for personal reflection or expression. This is true for either traditional or contemporary worship. On the other hand, there is a form of worship that emphasizes the personal at the expense of the communal, which would not necessarily be relevant either, because we are individuals within community. A balance must be found. Relevance speaks to the reality of our situations and in reality, we are both individuals in privacy and individuals in community. Worship that balances both the privacy and community elements within our natures will be meaningful worship.

A memorable worship experience occurred while leading a group of eighty high school youth on a choir tour. On one of the final days together, we had a communion worship service in the morning before traveling to our home congregation. Our eighty high school youth had Bible study groups that they participated in for an hour each day. At the communion service, each Bible study group performed a skit of their own creation, reflecting the lessons they learned. The atmosphere was far from reverent. The skits were hilarious yet meaningful. Often, we found ourselves literally rolling on the floor with laughter. After the last skit, we sang one song, and into holy communion we ventured. The mood quickly shifted. Perhaps we knew that this was our "last supper" together on tour and that had something to do with it, but as communion was distributed, there were many tears. The worship was powerful in its sense of community. The laughter and the tears created a lasting bond among us.

Worship must be personal yet communal. To be communal, worship must give worshipers opportunities for communal expressions of faith. Skits by various groups is a good idea. Every congregation has members who love to be on stage, youth and adults alike. Make sure the skits are appropriate, but a little laughter is a great way to feed the communal spirit. Yet to perform a skit, each skit participant makes a personal expression of faith. Personal yet communal.

At a liturgical worship service, it is more difficult to find an appropriate place for a skit, but it is possible and often desirable. Probably the most appropriate place for a skit at a traditional worship service would be at the announcement period. Instead of a few sentences about the youth pancake breakfast, why not encourage the youth to dress up like a pancake, syrup, butter, and a few utensils? The message will be both factual and utterly enjoyable. A word of caution. A skit is a sure winner for laughter and joy, but you cannot enjoy what you cannot hear. Make sure that either the participants project to the point of yelling, if need be, or they have a microphone. At a liturgical worship service it may also be possible to use a more "adult," and therefore more serious, skit at the reading of a lesson or as a portion of the pastor's sermon. Find the adults and youth who are animated and creative, and organize and encourage their efforts. A skit provides a wonderful avenue for developing a sense of community and, for those who participate, a sense of personal involvement and expression of faith. If a skit group can be formed, they can also be used as meaningful entertainment for social events and programs. Drama is a powerful tool to communicate the gospel. Drama takes advantage of the human ability of living an experience through others—the same power that Jesus used to communicate the gospel through parables.

Another meaningful way to provide an experience that is personal yet communal is through the use of a focal item. A candle can be a wonderful focal item at a Christmas Eve service if the fire marshall will allow it, although this is illegal in most cities. A lighted candle held by each adult provides a sense of personal worship that is hard to match. Yet if each worshiper takes the time to look around, or if they hold up their candles together, or even blow them out together, the communal spirit is also powerful. The focal item may be a lesson that is read together, or a litany that is recited together, or a hymn that is sung together, or even a cross made of palm leaf fragments on Palm Sunday; the list is endless, but the impact is the same. A focal point brings people together in community and yet, since participation is a personal choice, it also provides that needed personal dimension to worship. The wise worship leader will provide a worship experience that is personal yet communal.

Emotional Yet Instructional

The Scriptures say that "we do not know how to pray as we ought, but that very Spirit intercedes with sighs (or tears) too deep for words" (Rom. 8:26). The spirit of God works in us emotions that are worship experiences in their purest forms. Our worship experiences can encourage or discourage that demonstration of God's spirit. On the other hand, the apostle Paul, when dealing with the Corinthians on the subject of speaking in tongues, explains that emotional expressions of God's spirit are not beneficial to the larger group when emotion gets in the way of understanding. Emotional experiences move our hearts, but what we take with us to move our lives is what we learn in worship (1 Cor. 14). Worship, to be relevant, must be emotional yet instructional.

Our experience on choir tour was not only personal and communal, it was also emotional yet instructional. The emotion came from a movement of God's spirit. We cannot control that, nor can we duplicate the experience. However, it was the receiving of Holy Communion, and our knowledge that communion is prepared for by confession, that facilitated the emotional outpouring of God's spirit through tears. The most powerful emotional tools of worship will always be sacramental. A sacrament is "the means of God's grace." A sacrament utilizes an earthly element with spiritual significance—in Holy Communion it is the receiving of bread and wine, representing the broken body and spilt blood of Christ; in baptism it is the water that represents the washing and regeneration of our lives. Sacraments literally touch us. A sacrament is a hug and a kiss from God. Certainly God loves us always and deeply so, but as human beings, we need tangible representations of that love, like a hug or a kiss. For worship to evoke emotion, it must provide tangible representations of the gifts of God.

We must be more sensitive to the emotional elements of our sacraments. Receiving Holy Communion must be more than an assembly line. The encouragement of taking time for personal reflection would be more sensitive to the intent of the sacrament. Providing an opportunity for families to serve each other communion is powerful. "This is the body of Christ" says a mother to her son, or a husband to his wife. That's powerful! Every worship service should provide some kind of sacramental expression. If time limitations are a factor, try having Holy Communion at the close of worship. We have done this at our final worship service each Sunday, and this provides not only a time to receive communion, but often communicants linger for prayer, kneeling before the altar. This becomes also a time invaluable for pastoral care. For adults, as for the children, repetition is boring. Do not get so caught in a routine that the sacrament is drained of its emotional impact. Try to be creative.

With Holy Communion

* Take a time for personal, silent reflection.
* Have people turn to each other after confession, embrace each other and say "You are forgiven for Jesus' sake."
* Have a written confession that communicants takes to the altar with them.
* Receive the bread and wine in the pews or chairs as it is passed among the believers.
* Have the communicants read an absolution to themselves as they receive the bread and wine.

With Baptism

* Have worshipers place their hands in the baptismal waters as they leave (they may make the "sign of the cross") to renew their baptism.
* Have worshipers hold up their hand in a "blessing" gesture and repeat words of blessing on the baptized.
* Use readings and words of commitment to have worshipers renew their baptism during the worship service.
* Emphasize the work of the Holy Spirit in baptism with "fire" being a symbol of that baptism in God's spirit as a lone lit candle is passed among the worshipers.
* Start a "baptism banner" and have the names of the baptized printed on felt to be placed on the banner. Pass the felt-printed names around the congregation as each worshiper prays for the baptized.

This is just the beginning of the possibilities. The best possibilities will be the ideas your congregation develops from your situation as God speaks. The key is that emotion is facilitated when we are taken by surprise. The surprising is a product of creativity, and it is hindered by the routine. If your worship is so predictable that there is no room for the creative and the surprising, your worship is most likely without emotion. Is that what you want? Is that what God wants for you?

The question is not, "Is our worship contemporary or traditional?" Both contemporary and traditional worship services must guard against the evils of routine and stagnation. This is where worship becomes ritual without a heart. Boredom and worship are contradictory terms. Worship that is boring is not worship.

Rather, worship, when it is meaningful, ought to be considered an act of passionate love. Is one bored while making love? Not likely. Neither is it likely that worship can possibly take place effectively without emotion. Yet emotion is hollow when it is an end in itself. Emotion that is not beneficial is an artificial "high." Emotion by itself without tangible, beneficial qualities is like a drug or alcohol imposed high. It may be addictive and will be harmful, leaving the worshiper with a painful hangover or withdrawal from the experience.

Worship that is emotional without being beneficial can occur at a youth camp or retreat. The worship is often emotional, often bringing the worshiper to tears, but the act of worship is not carried over into the life of the believer. There is a withdrawal, with the youth becoming irritable and resentful that the reality within their life experiences, like their families, is not nearly as wonderful and freeing as the worship experienced.

The key to making worship emotional and yet beneficial is focus. Worship that is emotional and not beneficial is self-centered, even selfish. Worship that is emotional and also beneficial is other-centered. This is worship that reaches out to others, not worship that is an end in itself. Most often, this means changing very little that elicits the emotion, but rather, making sure that the emotion is not merely directed inward, but also outward—worship that finds the outside world an opportunity to express and complete the worship experience, worship that sees the outside world, not as an intrusion on the worship experience, but as an opportunity for the worship experience to be completed. A party is positive for those who attend, but the party is negative for those who are excluded. Worship that is emotional is an apparently meaningful worship, but we pervert worship's true significance when that emotion does not lead us out into the world to be a positive expression of the love of Christ.

Inspirational Yet Practical

Emotion can be and often is a private experience. Even when it is shared, it is most often the sharing of a private feeling. However, "inspiration" always includes a sense of God within the experience. Inspiration is often emotional, but everything that is emotional is not always inspiring. How does God inspire worship? How do we invite God to inspire our worship?

Inspirational worship is often symbolic and able to use symbols to elicit an emotional response. The experience of God cannot be put into a bottle, nor can it be quantified or qualified for mass distribution. The experience of the presence of God is most often an experience of symbols that project the worshiper personally into an experience of God, a truly spiritual experience. Symbols, by their nature, point beyond themselves. "For in hope we were saved. Now hope that is seen is not hope. For who hopes for what is seen? But if we hope for what we do not see, we wait for it with patience" (Rom. 8:24-25). The presence of God cannot be seen, but the essence of symbols is that they point us to the reality of God as an experienced hope. Symbols point us to the reality of hope in God because they point us to what cannot be seen. Worship that utilizes symbols is a patient, waiting style of worship filled with hope and expectancy.

A good example of patient, hopeful, expectant worship utilizing symbols is a candlelight worship service. Whether a large group or a small group worships, a candle as a symbol of the presence of God can touch our spirits and bring us into a relationship with the God we cannot see. The same effect can be accomplished using a campfire at a retreat or camping worship. Fire is a symbol of God's presence because it brings light and warmth; it calls people together. Fire and light from a candle burn, but are not quickly consumed. In a patient, quiet worship service, invite worshipers to share or think of how God has brought light into the darkness, warmth into the coldness of their lives. Let the worship leader or a few of the participating worshipers tell how God has been a power in his or her life that seems to give energy and yet is not consumed. The symbol of a burning light can allow the worshiper to experience the reality of God in many of God's attributes in a physical and tangible way.

Our scriptures are rich in symbols that can be used to invite a sense of the spiritual into our worship. While at a work camp in the Appalachian Mountains, the closing worship symbol was a rough-cut cross made from the scraps of wood that we used to repair the homes of the poor. For our closing worship, each worshiper took the hammer they used all week and used a nail to communicate a prayer concern or request. As the family who were the recipients of our labors were mentioned in their personal needs, it was clear that the nails driven into the cross represented our opportunity to bear the burdens of our new-found friends. It was a powerful, spiritual experience.

Sacramentally, the waters of baptism and the bread and wine of Holy Communion are obvious spiritual symbols, but let's not take the symbolism for granted. As in all of worship, boredom through mindless repetition is the great enemy. Let the waters of baptism touch not only the baptized but also other members of the family or congregation. Pour a portion of the water on a plant to be given to the baptized to emphasize the life-giving nature of the water. How about a foot-washing ceremony to emphasize the cleansing nature of the symbol of water through baptism? The United Methodist Church now includes a liturgy for foot washing (See *The United Methodist Book of Worship,* 1992). Symbols need explanation. Symbols need to be given to each worshiper or at least experienced by each worshiper to be significant in corporate worship. How else could the waters of baptism be used to make the symbolism come alive for each worshiper? The same may be said of the wine and bread within a communion service. The symbolism may be obvious, but fresh expressions of the obvious always add spiritual life to the worship.

Other biblical symbols can also add a sense of the Spirit to a worship service. Moses' rod, a shepherd's staff, a burning bush, a bright star, hands folded like a manger for the Christ Child, are all symbols that could be used to invite spirituality. Even secular symbols could be used effectively, but with more explanation and a sensitivity to placement. For example, a flag or a coin, a flower or an animal all have symbolic possibilities. Is not a children's sermon—using an object lesson—most often an experience in spiritual symbolism? Do we not often hear how meaningful those children's sermons are to adults? Children's sermons are popular and meaningful because of the use of symbolism to prod the worshipers' sense of participatory creativity—symbols that are creatively presented to engage the worshiper in the spiritual significance of everyday life.

The children's sermon points out the need for worship to be inspiring yet also practical. The symbol must have practical significance, without making it too blunt or literal. Just to say that a candle is a symbol for the Holy Spirit, but not to apply that symbolism, will not be inspirational because the symbolism has not been linked to something relevant or of practical significance to the worshiper. Rather, say that a candle is a symbol of the Holy Spirit because it gives off warmth and that warmth of God's love can burn away our sins. Then have the candle burn pieces of paper upon which each worshiper has written their confessed sins, pieces of paper pierced through nails sticking out from a wooden cross in the sanctuary. That gives symbolism practical significance. Even Jesus was frustrated with symbols like fasting or the places of honor in the marketplace for prayer that did not apply the symbolism to the worshiper's daily life. Impractical symbolism in worship is symbolism for the sake of symbolism, and it fosters religion without spirituality, form without power. Truly effective worship uses symbols for practical spirituality.

Another source for inspiring spirituality in worship is music. Music is symbolism for the ears and, like symbols for the eyes, it has the power to take us beyond ourselves. Music lifts our spirits and speaks to our emotions and it gives information to our minds. Music has a more specific spiritual impact, whereas visual symbols have a more general spiritual impact.

One of the great spiritual impacts that music is capable of producing is pure joy and excitement. Seldom do we look at a symbol and laugh or get excited. Although a symbol may elict emotion, it is more controlled or thoughtful emotion. Yet music has the specific ability to excite with less thoughtful contemplation. Also, a symbol may speak very strongly to some and never even impact someone standing next to him or her. Music, on the other hand, is contagious, and joy will either spread or die. Music will unite, or it will have no effect at all. Where music unites, where music is contagious, music has powerful spiritual implications.

What is the golden key that can unlock the spiritual power of music in worship? Again, guard against boredom, but with a slightly different intention. What is boring about music is exactly what makes it powerful. Music goes against the general rule that repetition is boring. The most powerful spiritual music is repetitious. Usually some great truth is repeated over and over. Like; the battle is the Lord's, what a friend we have in Jesus, beautiful savior, lift high the cross or any number of other examples. The basic truth of powerful Christian music must be repeated again and again to be effective. With this understanding, spiritually uplifting music must be simple, even repetitious, and neither complicated nor long. Where repetition in music becomes negative is where the same kind of music is used time and time again. Hammer home the message, but do not use the same hammer at each opportunity. Even the best music can become old. On the other hand, complicated music, which is music that has too many verses, too many lyrics or that is difficult to learn, will never reach the spirit either.

When music is simple yet powerful, uncomplicated yet deep in meaning, then music is spiritual yet practical. Practical music is music that we take home with us. More important practical music hits home to us. The message is simple. The spirit is contagious.

Prayer is another element that can bring about the power of spirituality and yet be practical in worship. We do the people of God a great disservice if we continue to pray for them. Spectator prayer is elementary prayer and it is time to add spiritual depth to our prayer in worship. The golden key is to allow the people of God the time and opportunity to pray themselves.

Often, what can be done in a small setting cannot be done in a larger setting. In a small setting, the worshipers can be asked to pray out loud as the Spirit moves within them.

Two problems can arise. First, it may be difficult to get people to vocalize their prayers if they are not used to doing so. Often, having one or two people asked ahead to pray out loud will encourage the prayers of others. Also encourage one-word prayers that are easy to speak out. For example, pray "Dear Lord, we thank you for the following that we now raise before you: _____."
The congregation would have been instructed to share a single word or phrase that depicts their thankfulness. The same may be done in offering prayers for people we love and are concerned about. "Lord, we name the following loved ones who we commend to your loving care, knowing that their needs are more apparent to you than they are even to themselves: _____."

A litany may also be effective. For example, instructions are given that we are going to pray for the ministries of the church. Each individual prays, "Lord bless the witness of _____," filling in the blank with names of individuals or committees or projects. After each personal contribution to the prayer, the congregation as a whole will be instructed to pray: "Lord bless our ministry." This combines the personal with the corporate in a powerful way. A final suggestion would be to have individuals come forward who are in special need or having a special celebration. Needs include sickness, personal-relational problems, fears and the like. Celebrations include birthdays, anniversaries, retirements and the like. When they come forward, they can kneel before an altar or hold a lit candle as their specific needs or celebrations are prayed for. Celebrations do not mix well with needs, but there can be a time in each worship service for both. Just try not to pray for a cancer victim while simultaneously noting a little boy who is celebrating a birthday. Pray for celebrations near the announcements or the offering, and pray for needs following the sermon or at the time for the prayers of the church.

The above are prayer suggestions for worship in a smaller group. In a larger group, intimacy may be more difficult. Prayer in a larger group can be accomplished through a prayer request card. Many larger congregations use the prayer request card, but then fail to actually pray for the requests in the worship service. Even simply to collect the cards and pray for the heap of cards on the altar would at least acknowledge the requests and their significance. A system could be worked out where ushers collect prayer requests at the time of the offering and those requests are immediately separated from the offering and typed on a prayer request sheet. If the process can be accomplished in fifteen to twenty minutes, the requests could be prayed for at the conclusion of the service. Another technique in large group settings to get more personal with prayer is to invite a show of hands or some other gesture to indicate a particular type of need. The worship leader may instruct, "Please raise your hand if we may pray for a particular concern you have, a trouble you are going through or a health problem that is hurting you." Those with raised hands may be prayed for and someone close to that person may be asked to place their hand on that person as a symbol of concern. In a large group, a time of silence could be used to have the people pray silently for something or someone that needs those prayers.

Spiritual Yet Tangible

Relevance is no more powerfully communicated in worship than when the worship service leads each worshiper to a change of life-style. Worship must not only comfort the afflicted, it must also afflict the comfortable to be meaningful.

The sermon or the message is the best place to bring the relevance of the lesson and the season into our homes and lives. Preachers should ask themselves the question, "What have I said that will impact the lives of those who hear?" Here, some of the other dimensions of relevant worship could be used. Worship that is relevant is:

> Personal yet communal
> Emotional yet beneficial
> Inspiring yet practical
> Spiritual yet tangible

Everything on the left is "spiritual" worship. Everything on the right is "tangible" worship. Spiritual worship is personal, emotional, and inspiring. Tangible worship is communal, beneficial, and practical. Some preachers outline their sermons so they can literally be taken home. The message can be challenging and a commitment could be asked for and recorded.

For example, the sermon may be on prayer. The sermon could invite the worshiper to make a commitment to pray daily, giving a seven-day devotional as an instrument of prayer. The congregation could then be instructed to take a devotional only if they are committed to use it, each day faithfully. If five hundred worshipers attend and two hundred fifty-six take the daily devotion, that is tangible worship.

Another tangible opportunity for worship is to pass out grocery bags with a list of the needs of a local food shelf. The sermon could be on feeding the hungry and how Jesus explained that as we "did it" to the least of these we did it to him. A very spiritual message. But the grocery bags make the message tangible. The message is literally taken home with us and a response is invited, even expected.

What is the challenge? How can the challenge be made tangible and quantifiable? Relevant worship is spiritual yet tangible. God empowers us to make a commitment. Worship has to make a difference in our lives to be relevant.

Worship That Welcomes

Worship that welcomes must also be relevant. Relevant worship that welcomes is worship that welcomes the visitor. How can worship be relevant to the visitor? A worship that welcomes is:

> Easy to learn
> Clearly stated without assumptions
> Initiates a relationship
> In tune with the sensitivities of potential visitors

Easy to Learn

First, a welcoming worship is easy to learn. This does not mean the worship is childish or simple, but the worship does recognize that the great themes of the Christian faith are profound in their simplicity. A way to look at this truth in the sports world is to emphasize fundamentals. Without "fundamentals," even a professional athlete will fail. How much more important it is for visitors to be given the fundamentals of the Christian faith in order for them to begin their relationship with a church. Accordingly, it is important that each worship service have a definable, yet fundamental theme. A worship service is easy to learn if its theme is clearly stated and emphasized throughout the worship service. The worship's theme needs to be like a golden thread holding the service together and giving it continuity. That same thread should be emphasized in the sermon, with the sermon being held together by the theme. Transitions between elements within the service should also emphasize the theme and how one element speaks to the theme and leads to another. As people leave worship, worshipers should be able to speak the theme to themselves and carry it with them throughout the week. Repetition is the mother of learning, and where a theme is repeated, it will be learned. The simpler the theme, the more likely the theme will be remembered. The more creative the presentation of the theme, in its various possibilities, the more likely the worship will be enjoyable and foundational to the worshipers' faith and, in particular, the faith of a visitor.

Clearly Stated without Assumptions

A simple yet profound message is best presented in a clear, yet uncomplicated manner. A welcoming worship clearly states its message without making assumptions. The story is told of a traveling vacuum cleaner salesman whose technique of sales was to get his foot in the door of a prospective home and throw a bag of manure on the entrance carpet before the resident had a chance to object. The salesman approached a house, knocked on the door, and, as a little old lady answered the door, he threw the bag of manure on the carpet. Before the little old lady could object, the salesman explained: "Lady, this vacuum is so powerful and I have so much confidence in its ability that I believe this vacuum will pick up every speck of this manure or I will personally get on my hands and knees and pick up every speck by hand." To which the little old lady replied, "Well, come on in, we don't have any electricity." How much trouble we can get ourselves into by having false assumptions! Don't "assume" anything. Check it out.

What are the possible assumptions we may make in a worship service that will hamper and even prevent a visitor from participating in a worship service? We too often assume that everyone who worships with us:

* knows what to do with their children
Is there Sunday school going on?
Where is the nursery?

Is the nursery a quality place?

Are children welcome in the worship?

Can children be children in worship?

* knows the layout of the church campus

Is there special parking for visitors?

Where is the sanctuary?

Where is the nursery?

Where is the pastor's office?

Where can I find directions and ask questions?

Where is my child's Sunday school class?

Where are the restrooms?

* knows how to take steps to become involved in the church

What is the purpose of a visitor card, does it obligate me in any way?

Can I stay inconspicuous until I'm ready to commit myself further?

What are the educational opportunities and, more important what are the educational obligations and expectations?

If I were to become a member, would I have to take classes or be rebaptized or stand in front of the church or support the church in any of a number of ways?

What are the benefits of membership?

What are the benefits of remaining a visitor?

* knows the nuts and bolts of a particular worship service

When do I stand up, sit down, or kneel?

Do I know this music?

Is the music easy to learn?

How do I receive communion?

Is the service in the bulletin, or do I need to balance a book with the bulletin?

What are the worship gestures and are they necessary or optional?

Is there more than the worship service in the bulletin, and can I easily distinguish between advertisements, calendars, and the actual service?

How can I find out the worship times and the worship styles at the various times?

Is this worship best suited for my tastes?

How long will this worship service last?

Are there special worship times and styles throughout the year?

To make a worship clearly stated without unanswered assumptions, these issues must be taken into consideration and the questions answered. The questions must be answered creatively. If you choose to answer the questions with printed material, another question must be answered. Namely, is what is printed read and if read, will it be understood? The best answer may be to pair guests with tour guides, or sponsors. Generally a personal touch is the most effective touch because questions can be answered as they arise. Most churches address visitors after they have worshiped, if at all. Why not train the evangelism team to meet, greet, and answer the questions of visitors as they arrive on the church campus? Not only could questions be answered and assumptions met, but also, visitors could be introduced to other members who have similar interests or backgrounds.

Initiates a Relationship

Initiating a relationship is hard work. Why do we ask our visitors to do the hard work of initiating a relationship with the church when the church can train its members to initiate relationships? As mentioned, that first opportunity to initiate a relationship is prior to worship. Many churches enlist greeters, but few take the greeting a step further and actually initiate relationships. It can be done, and to do so would be very effective in bringing the visitor into the fellowship.

Still, this should not cause us to neglect opportunities for home visits to initiate relationships. Those home visits are most effective and less offensive if the visits are done by the preaching pastor. A senior pastor of a seven thousand member congregation boasted that there was not one family whose home he had not been in. That's the majority of what he did. He preached and he visited the congregation. It is possible to train lay people to do these visits, but it is a more difficult visit because a lay visitor is considered a stranger, and the preaching pastor has already established a relationship through the preaching message. Use trained lay people to welcome the visitor to the church campus, and use the pastor(s) to visit in homes.

Programs can also initiate relationships with visitors if the programs foster small group interaction. There is only one relationship fostered at a lecture. The relationship with the lecturer. If a relationship is to be long-term, it must be introduced by programs and fostered by small groups. Small groups will be addressed in greater detail in chapter 6.

In Tune with the Sensitivities of Potential Visitors

Who visits your church? What are your visitors looking for? What do the visitors react to positively, and what do the visitors react to negatively? When a group of new members enters a congregation, we usually take great efforts to introduce them to the church and its teachings. We miss the opportunity when we do not spend just as much time and effort to learn from those new members. What can we learn from our new members?

* What does the church do effectively?
* What does the church do ineffectively?
* Does the church meet your needs?
* Does the church fail to meet certain needs?
* What is the perceived focus of the church?
* What members of the church have been influential in making you feel welcomed?

Learn from visitors and new members if you want to reach visitors and add more new members. This should be done thoroughly and systematically. Use small group discussions, questionnaires, personal interviews and the like. A welcoming church is a growing church. A growing church welcomes effectively.

6

SMALL GROUP MINISTRY: FACT OR FICTION—REALITY OR MYTH

Small group ministry is sometimes promised to be the savior of congregations in the 1990s. Small group ministry promises exponential growth. Small groups produce more groups which, in turn, produce more groups. It is pyramid thinking that can have all the trappings of the "get rich quick" pyramid sales schemes. The promises are always greater than the results—apart from a few, often very few, notable exceptions. Let's separate the facts from the fiction, the reality from the myths.

Fact: Effective small group ministry is dependent upon quality leadership and that leadership is in desperately short supply.

Fact: A good leader makes a good small group.

Fact: Leadership is not a genetic trait. Leadership is learned.

Fact: You can only teach so much to a potential leader. The most important leadership training will come with experience and, most important of all, a deep hunger to learn.

Fact: Leadership is draining. You can't drink from an empty cup. Leadership doubles the time commitment to a small group. A leader must spend at least as much time in preparation for a small group as in the group itself.

Fact: The most important benefit of a small group is not the learning of information but the building of relationships. Therefore, small group leaders should not be trained to give lectures, but to build and facilitate discussions on information with an emphasis on self-disclosure and enhancing skills in interpersonal relationships.

Fact: Small groups are motivational because they speak primarily to the heart and only secondarily do they speak to the head. The opposite is true of a large group, which primarily speaks to the head and only secondarily speaks to the heart. The heart motivates and inspires. The head teaches and informs. Therefore, the small group leader may have very different skills and be a very different personality type than the person who we may first associate with the word "leader."

Fact: Small groups are time and commitment intensive and many people will not join a small group because of the time and commitment cost. If 40 percent of your membership are in a small group, they deserve an "A" for commitment.

Fact: Small groups are based on intimacy and not privacy. Our society is becoming more and more private and the promise that small groups are the answer to ministry in the 1990s may be more myth than reality, if the trend toward privacy, aided by technology, continues.

Fact: People are often more anxious to join a small group that is both discussion and task oriented. Small groups that probe the thoughts of the participants are just one type of small group. Many small groups can be effective if they unite the participants around a task and only secondarily, but importantly, are discussion based.

But beware! Small group ministry is often shrouded in fiction.

Fiction: Small group ministry is easy.

Fiction: Small group ministry has built-in growth.

Fiction: Once a small group is formed it will always exist.

Fiction: Small group ministry is always "quality" ministry.

Fiction: Everyone is interested in small group ministry and will join a group given the right circumstances.

Fiction: Almost anyone can lead a small group. The most effective way to begin a small group ministry is to make a decision as to where small group ministry would be most effective and recruit and train leaders.

Fiction: Once a small group is formed, it requires little, if any, maintenance. This is the most destructive fiction of all!

First, realize that small group ministry is not the best way to pass on information. Oddly, most church small groups are Bible studies, and if the intention is to learn what the Bible says, this may not be the method of choice. Obviously if the small group leader is an expert in biblical studies, he or she or can lead a small group and pass on the information, but would it not be better to pass that information on in a large group so that many more may be influenced by the expertise? On the other hand, how can a small group multiply if the small group is dependent upon the expertise of the leader? Does it not waste the expertise of scholars to put them in charge of a small group?

Second, realize that a small group ministry is not the best vehicle to entertain participants. Again, the question is not, "Can an entertainer effectively entertain a small group?" but rather the question is, "Do we waste the ability of entertainers in a small group setting when they could be just as entertaining in a large group setting?"

Although a small group may not be an ideal place to pass on the knowledge of an expert or the thrills of an entertainer, it does have a wonderful ability to promote intimacy among its members. A small group is not a place to share knowledge nor the excitement of entertainment, but it is an ideal place to share interpersonal intimacy. Focus on this strength.

People today thirst for intimacy, but it is so rare that many do not even know how barren their lives are without it. We live in a secular world where "secular" has become synonymous for cold, private individualism. We value tasks over people, results over feelings. We have replaced love with sex. We have replaced entertainment with crude violence. We see leadership as the insensitive giving of orders. We are strangers not only to the world around us, but even to our own families. Marriages are often ended with the harsh reality that we are "together alone." Feelings are hidden. Caring is rare. We feel afraid before we feel compassion as we meet the homeless. We feel disgust rather than sympathy when we are confronted with the poor. Small group ministry can bring about intimacy, but are we too lost in the submersion of feelings within the confines of this secular world to even see the needs we have for intimacy? Beyond recognizing our need for intimacy, will we invest the time demanded of a small group ministry to meet this ill-defined need?

Because small group ministry effectively meets our need for intimacy, when small group ministry works, it can have powerful effects. But because our need for intimacy is hidden and not valued by our society, the risk of the failure of a small group ministry is also great. The key to effective small group ministry is leadership, leadership, leadership. A small group is only as effective as its leadership. Even if the participants are utterly uncooperative, a good leader can bring about positive intimacy. But leadership in a small group requires entirely different skills than would be found in a large group leader. Contrast the leadership skills of a small group leader versus a large group leader:

Small Group Leader	*Large Group Leader*
Good Listener	Good Speaker
Feelings Communicated	Knowledge and Talent Communicated
Centered on the Other	Centered on the Self
Informal Spirit	Formal Spirit
Feeds on the Unexpected	Feeds on the Preparations
Seeks Two-way Communication	Seeks One-way Communication
Subjective	Objective
Speaks to the Heart	Speaks to the Head or Senses

Leadership is not a simple subject. Leadership does not "come naturally"; it must be learned and tested. We will look into the subject of leadership development in the next chapter, but for now, simply hold up the fact that a small group leader is very different from a large group leader, and a large group leader is the leader our culture cultivates and admires.

Intimacy is the primary benefit of effective small group ministry. Intimacy is most influenced in the small group by the skill of its leader. However, the format of the small group can also assist or hinder the development of small group intimacy. For example, we have often found that some women's groups, such as circles, destroy intimacy through regimented and formal procedures. When visiting a circle, I am amazed at the formality. It is almost like someone has given the participants a recipe for being together, and they measure out each facet meticulously and objectively. The snacks are served with the best dishes and an obvious effort is made to make everything look "pretty." The opening prayer is read, not freely spoken from the heart. The Bible study is a process of reading scriptures, answering questions about scriptures, and making observations about how the Bible speaks to modern situations. The meeting closes with the Lord's Prayer and everyone leaves talking about the unimportant with cold objectivity. What's wrong? Formality and regimented procedures create a sense of distance and not intimacy. Prayer that is read is an exercise in reading, not the groanings of the heart. Scripture studies that center around factual information rather than a discussion of personal issues promotes learning at the expense of the heart. If you want to feed the head and not the heart, find an expert or a professional and use a large group format with plenty of visual aids. If you want to feed the heart, use a format that promotes intimacy through personal sharing and self-disclosure.

The principles of intimacy within a small group setting are:

(1) A relaxed, informal atmosphere
(2) Self-disclosure, not fact-finding

(3) Discussion, not lecture

(4) Participatory prayer

(5) Confidentiality or safety issues

(6) Personalized ritual

(7) Commitment

A Relaxed, Informal Atmosphere

To create a relaxed, informal atmosphere within a small group setting is to first pay attention to the physical circumstances of the room. A participant's living room is often ideal, while a church classroom is the most difficult place to elicit a feeling of intimacy. Chairs should be in a circle and never in rows. Make sure the circle is as truly a circle if possible so that each participant can clearly see the face of every other participant. Dress informally and even consider sitting on the floor instead of on furniture. Have the circle be tight enough so that each participant can easily touch the other participants next to them in the circle. The lighting is best when it is subdued and not bright or dim, especially where older adults may be present. Make sure there are no distracting noises or activities to draw attention away from the group. Even consider meeting in a cramped area rather than a large area with distractions or too much space. When I work with youth, I have met in large closets and even bathrooms rather than in an open area with distractions.

Self-Disclosure, Not Fact-Finding

A small group's greatest strength is its ability to promote intimacy, and the circumstance within that small group that is most important in promoting intimacy is self-disclosure. There is no intimacy without self-disclosure, and discussion is the primary vehicle for self-disclosure. A small group takes on the characteristics of a living organism. Every member of a living organism must take part in the life of that organism. If even one member of that organism fails to take part, it lives as a wounded organism, injured, unhealthy, and having its life threatened. It happens again and again. A small group can be only as intimate as its most hesitant participant is willing to risk self-disclosure. Often, the leader will set the tone for self-disclosure. Often, the leader's skill will be tested in soliciting the self-disclosure of each of the group's members. If just one of the group's members refuses to disclose feelings and thoughts, the entire group will become inhibited. On the other hand, if the leader can set the tone for intimate self-disclosure of feelings and thoughts, and each participant follows that lead, the small group can become the most important social relationship in the life of its participants. Family, spouse, lifelong friendships can pale in importance to be a fellow member of an intimate small group. However, this is not to say that all intimacies are appropriate for a small group setting. When self-disclosure of a concern or issue may hurt yourself or someone else, it is too great a responsibility to share that intimacy with a group of people. Further, some intimacies are too difficult for a small group to process and should be the exclusive domain of a single friend or perhaps a professional counselor. Wisdom and mature judgment must be exercised in determining if or when a shared intimacy is appropriate for a small group. Is the shared intimacy beyond the group's capability of being able to safely and effectively take on the responsibility of the information? That is not an easy question to answer. Each small group member and, in particular, the small group leader, must take great pains in answering that question based on an evaluation of the gravity of the information shared and the character of the group.

If a small group is going to be effective, it must be self-disclosing rather than fact-finding; it must be willing to share feelings rather than facts; it must be willing to share thoughts and opinions rather than information.

From a spiritual dimension, this is translated into the open sharing of doubts, not the sharing of the tenets of faith. It means the sharing of fears, not acts of faith. It means the sharing of spiritual weaknesses and failings, not spiritual victories. Self-disclosure takes Jesus' instructions seriously that the first will be last and the last will be first. The sharing of the negative in terms of the self with an attitude of searching and vulnerability is the most conducive spiritual sharing a group can promote.

Discuss, Not Lecture

An effective small group is designed to promote self-disclosure and through self-disclosure, intimacy will result. Moreover, self-disclosure is not possible where the communication style is that of a lecture. The communication style that is most conducive to self-disclosure is discussion, but may not be limited to discussion. Also, some types of discussion promote more self-disclosure than others. For example, some discussion centers around factual material. It is hard to "discuss" facts, other than an obvious recounting of the details. Many Bible studies are fact-finding adventures that make them of little value to the self-disclosure possibilities within a small group. On the other hand, if the discussion is on feelings, opinions, life experiences or the like, the discussion is much more profitable to the life of the small group. Discussions can be led by asking open-ended questions such as "Describe the most destructive thing that's ever happened to you," or they can be led by asking questions that are closed, which can be answered by a simple yes or no, such as, "Have you been destructive today?" Open-ended questions that are as broad as possible promote discussion better than closed questions that are narrow. Favorite open-ended and broad questions are:

(1) What's the best thing that's ever happened in your past?
(2) What's the best thing happening now?
(3) What's the best thing that could happen in your future?
(4) What's the worst thing that's happened in your past?
(5) What's the worst thing that's happening now?
(6) What's the worst thing that could happen in your future?

These questions are awesome in their power to elicit self-disclosure. I have used these questions in a group as small as four or five, and we talked for hour upon hour, through laughter and tears. Discussion can be dominated by one or two participants, or worse, by the leader. Discussion as such becomes a lecture and destructive to the workings of the small group. All participants must participate in the discussion for it to be effective. This often is dependent upon the skills and sensitivity of the leader. However, anyone in the small group could be sensitive to this dynamic. Those who have much to say must be quieted. Those who have little to say must be encouraged. No one is to be judged for what they say. Everyone is to be encouraged for what they say. Effective small group discussion includes everyone for about an equal amount of time. Make this expectation clear at the beginning of the group with its reasoning, and the participants will seek to honor it.

Participatory Prayer

Spiritual intimacy with others is defined by the quality of small group prayer. Prayer opens the human spirit as the human spirit opens itself to the presence of God. Prayer is the vehicle for spiritual intimacy within a small group. Prayer can add a spiritual dimension to intimacy that makes human intimacy just a brief, pale taste of true spiritual intimacy. But just any prayer will not lead to intimacy.

Prayer, like the communication within a small group, must be primarily motivated by self-disclosure and take the form of a discussion with God. With this idea in mind, encourage the sharing of personal feelings and needs. Ideally, each participant can share those personal feelings and needs verbally in prayer, but often this will not take place without gradually working into it. Praying out loud in public, even within a small close-knit group, can be very intimidating. But there are techniques to ease a small group into participatory prayer.

Step 1. If the members of the small group are hesitant to participate in prayer, the first step is to talk about prayer. If it is difficult to pray out loud, discuss the petitions for prayer. What are your needs, your concerns, your fears, your troubles? What are your joys, your victories, your accomplishments? These are items for prayer. Keep a prayer list. If it is too much to ask for to pray out loud, then for a time pray silently for the petitions discussed. Encourage the participating to pray daily for the discussed petitions. The first step is to bring prayer concerns to remembrance. It may take a long time to share these concerns. Do not let this step turn into gossip, but allow plenty of time to share personal burdens and joys.

Step 2. The next step to promote participatory prayer is to harvest utterances of prayer from the participants. These prayers can be harvested by several means. Try asking each member to pray a one-word prayer. For example, say, "Let's express our thanks to God by saying out loud one thing or person or experience or circumstance that we are thankful to God for" or "Let's pray to God for a blessing on each of us, and all I want you to do is to call out the name of the person on your right at one time during the silent time of this prayer." Another possibility in prompting a spoken prayer by each participant is to give them a prayer to read with a "fill in the blank" space. Like, "Lord Jesus I need your help with *(name)*" or "Lord, I am most surrounded by your peace and love when *(situation)*. I thank you Jesus." Do not only have each participant read a prayer. The prayer must have a blank space where they can fill in the blank with a personal petition. Intimacy is a product of self-disclosure. Pass around a symbol, a cross, a dove, or a flower and ask each member of the group to pray using that focal point. The possibilities are endless and each possibility should be tailored to the character of the particular small group.

Step 3. Once the group has been initiated to speaking words or phrases of prayer in a more controlled setting, it is now time to take the leap of faith into encouraging the participants to pray in their own words for specific people, events, or circumstances. First, discuss possible prayer requests and then assign a request to each participant or ask the participants to volunteer to pray for the requests. Another possibility is to have everyone share a prayer concern and have everyone pray for the person on their right or left with the request as the focal point of the prayer. Often, people are more likely to pray when there is a candle used as a focal point and the rest of the meeting room is darkened. Encourage participatory prayer at the beginning of each meeting and its close. Maybe begin by asking someone to pray for the group and close by having everyone participate in prayer. Prayer is spiritual intimacy in its purest form.

Confidentiality or Safety Issues

From the very beginning of a small group, it must be made clear that any personal information discussed is confidential. Nothing that is said in the group should be considered common knowledge. All information must be considered confidential. One of the quickest ways to destroy a group is to betray a trust. Confidentiality must be the foundation for self-disclosure. If the leader could begin the meeting by communicating something in confidence, that could set the tone for the small group meetings from that point on. The general rule is that a small group will be only as intimate as its leadership is willing to be, and if the leader communicates something in trust from the very beginning, that can illustrate the willingness of the leader to risk and put to the test the confidentiality of the group. But I again must emphasize that there are some intimacies within everyone's life that are not to be shared in a small group regardless of how sacred the confidentiality.

Safety is a product of the group's confidentiality. Many people feel the need to be intimate, but they most often express that need in privacy with a small number of people. We can be hurt by information about ourselves that is misused or taken lightly. Always consider personal information as the most precious gift one can receive from someone. When the gift is given with love, it should be received with love. To feel safe is to feel accepted. To be accepted with information about ourselves that is not common knowledge is to feel safe and affirmed. That is intimacy, the glue that holds a small group together.

Personalized Ritual

One of the ways to promote intimacy is to promote ritual, and ritual that is personalized can be a powerful source of intimacy, especially in a small group. Lighting a candle or holding a candle that is passed around a group can help to facilitate self-disclosure and can help to promote intimacy. A cross that is passed around the group can help each member of the group talk about something they confess as a sin or mistake in their life. A painting, a nail, a lamb stuffed animal, or a baby's diaper can each elicit memories, and those memories can be shared and explained. A meal, a foot washing, a laying on of hands can be group activities that promote intimacy through self-disclosure. Everyone is asked to participate, everyone focuses on an object or activity, and the ritual can be a creative and effective tool for small group formation and development.

Commitment

It is almost impossible to develop a continuing small group without commitment. A small group must meet regularly and at least every other week, preferably every week, ideally forty-five to forty-eight weeks annually. The group will suffer if even one or two fail to come at any given meeting. It is better not to have someone in the group if they cannot be committed to come virtually every time the group meets. A small group is like a living organism, and when one member fails to come, it is like an open wound where the life of the group is drained. It is better to terminate a small group rather than let the group die from apathy and guilt feelings.

7

LEADERSHIP, LEADERSHIP, LEADERSHIP

Providing excitement for children's ministries will not happen without good leadership. Youth ministry that utilizes our youth to minister to one another must be initiated by church leadesrhip that equips youth for this work. Parents must reestablish their leadership roles within the family for the family to be restored to its needed influence in the lives of its children. Reaching the poor and the powerless with new programs and ministries will not take place without leadership powering these efforts. In short, reaching new generations of believers cannot take place without leadership, leadership, leadership.

Christian leadership is very different from secular leadership. True enough, it is often hard to distinguish between secular leadership and Christian leadership as it is represented in our churches, but, nonetheless, the distinction is biblical and significant.

In Matthew 20, the mother of the sons of Zebedee came to Jesus with her two sons, asking that they sit at Jesus' right and left hands in his kingdom. Jesus replies, "You do not know what you are asking. Are you able to drink the cup that I am about to drink?" They say they are able, and Jesus explains, "You will indeed drink my cup, but to sit at my right hand and at my left, this is not mine to grant, but it is for those for whom it has been prepared by my Father" (Matt. 20:23). The other ten disciples are upset by this apparent power play, but Jesus explains the essence of true Christian leadership by stating, "You know that the rulers of the Gentiles lord it over them, and their great ones are tyrants over them. It will not be so among you; but whoever wishes to be great among you must be your servant, and whoever would be first among you must be your slave; just as the Son of Man came not to be served but to serve, and to give his life a ransom for many" (Matt. 20:25-28).

We live in a time when many of us are abdicating our leadership responsibilities. Take parenting, for example. Is not parenting a leadership responsibility? Yet parents more and more are giving up that leadership responsibility to so-called experts. Parents want teachers to lead their children in learning, churches to lead their children in moral development, coaches to lead their children in physical development, counselors to lead their children in emotional development, and TV sets to lead their children in all of the above, plus entertain their children. Very little is left of the parenting leadership role.

Take the husband-wife relationship as another example. The greatest marital problem I have found today is among couples who feel alone when they are together. Married couples spend time with each other, but fail to take responsibility for leading the relationship in a purposeful and meaningful way. Careers often dictate and dominate schedules while family relationships suffer. Is this the priority of our Christian community? How many would say that their careers are more important than their families? Very few! How many act as if their careers are more important than their families? The vast majority! Why? Because we are letting outside forces rule our lives while we fail to lead our personal lives according to our priorities. It is a leadership problem when husbands and wives grow apart, taking each other for granted. If a husband or wife is going to have an extramarital affair, it will most often be with a work partner. Why? It is at work that husbands and wives expend most of their energies, where the leadership role is accepted. At home, that leadership role lacks commitment, energy, and direction. It appears that many couples expect a good marriage to simply happen, when a good marriage must be a product of hard work, with both the husband and wife taking leadership roles in the relationship.

The church, too, suffers from a leadership drought. Professional leaders are in place, often a governing board is in place, there are teachers for the children, but beyond these exceptions, the church has developed very few leaders. If we have in mind secular leadership, a few leaders are enough. This is leadership for the many by the few, which remains to this day as Jesus explained the nature of Gentile leadership, ". . . the rulers of the Gentiles lord it over them, and their great ones are tyrants over them . . . ." This "Gentile" leadership is the only leadership we tend to have in the church today. Leadership that is not dependent upon the exercise of authority is the leadership that Jesus advocates—servant leadership. A servant leader can serve one or many. There is room for everyone to take on a servant leadership role in the church. We can only have a few leaders of authority in the church and those few must agree or there is inevitable conflict. If the church's leadership is in conflict, we can often venture to assume the leadership style is authoritarian. Servant leadership promotes harmony. Conflict is minimized where the leadership of the church focuses on service rather than authority.

Servant leadership does not come naturally. We do not learn servant leadership in secular society. Servant leadership must be taught. Servant leadership is a role that every member of the church can and should embrace.

Small Group, Not Large Group Leadership

Small group leadership is primarily servant leadership with a touch of authoritarian leadership. Effective large group leadership usually is largely authoritarian leadership with a touch of servant leadership. A good small group leader will be skilled in servant leadership, but will also know when to use a stronger and more direct approach—like a seasoning in the small group stew, it is not the meat and potatoes, but essential in its subtle influence. A good large group leader will be skilled in the authoritarian approach—not dictatorial, but nonetheless strong, not callous, but nonetheless willing to stand by an unpopular decision for the sake of general health.

Small group leaders have four basic leadership roles:

(1) Catalysts for the group's energy and ideas
(2) Shepherds for those hurting in the group
(3) Referees promoting fairness and equity
(4) Environmentalists

Catalysts

Small group leaders never overlead or overplan. A small group leader realizes that the best leadership will come from within the group. Ideas, direction, goals, objectives, decisions, focus, energy and the like, must come from the group and not the leader of the group. This means that the group leader serves as a catalyst or facilitator for the group's activity. This is both easier and more difficult than it sounds. First, the small group leader, where the primary purpose is to share feelings and emotions, cannot overplan. The planning must be a product of the group's interaction. It sounds easier to plan less, but for many, that can be very difficult. Planning less means more can go "wrong" because predetermined agendas, with predetermined questions, cannot be used. More is left to the unknown, and the unknown is always fearful. I have always found that when the silence of an unplanned portion of a group's time becomes awkward and oppressive, it is always best to appeal to the group's experiences. A group of Sunday school teachers was learning how to use material that was experientially based. The material used a limited number of Bible verses and stories, with the majority of the time spent in games or activities that illustrated the biblical wisdom. Following the game or activity, a discussion was led by the Sunday school teacher on what was learned. This was the unplanned portion of the lesson, and a few of the teachers were extremely uncomfortable, and felt inadequate to lead these discussions. Apparently the teachers were unprepared to handle a discussion that went beyond their own thoughts. For example, one teacher told of a session on "Jesus the Light of the World," where each student was to walk around the church property and find sources of light. When the children returned, the question to be discussed was how these discovered light sources are similar to and teach about Jesus as the light of the world. The Sunday school teachers felt that the children couldn't get the connection. They had some ideas, but it seemed the children drew blanks. It was suggested to relate to the children's experience of being in the dark. When were you in the dark? What happened? How did the dark make you feel? What can make being in the dark a positive experience? These questions helped the teachers to see that discussion is best facilitated not with abstract concepts, but rather, simple accounts of experiences. Experiences are often personal and private. A good small group leader cannot plan the content of these experiences, but these experiences are vital to the group's interaction when the purpose of the group is to share feelings and emotions.

The temptation of a teacher in a small group learning experience will be to have a predetermined plan that leaves no room for creativity and the unexpected. "Tangents" off the subject are seen as unproductive, but for those skilled in small group leadership, tangents are God's gifts from the Holy Spirit, to be treasured and explored for all they are worth.

To be an effective catalyst, a deep appreciation for the unknown, the unexpressed, the unplanned must be developed. "What unforeseen ways did God lead our group today?" Someone once told me that they do not believe in coincidences. To them, a coincidence is a gift from God that someone of faith has not recognized. To them, a coincidence may be a "God incidence," or an opportunity for God to speak that must be listened to and explored. This is difficult to teach, but an invaluable sinsitivity to learn. So much pain in our lives is caused by people who cannot accept what they have because it is not a part of their predetermined plans. So much joy in life can be discovered where we listen first and talk second, where we see the unexpected as an opportunity, not a nuisance. This is not to say that all coincidences are "God incidences," but this is an understanding of life where God does care and does interact with us. There are evil circumstances that occur that God has not part in controlling and others that simply are coincidences.

Shepherd

A small group leader must also be prepared to "get down and get personal." A servant serves. A shepherd nurtures and protects. A small group leader is caring and warm, open and generous. Everyone who comes to a small group has hidden pains and troubles. The only way to encourage the sharing of those pains and troubles is to be open and communicate one's own pains and troubles. Respect the boundaries of others, but literally lead the way by example. The group will share their troubles to the degree that its leader will share his or her troubles. Intimacy is never effectively solicited in a group, it must be modeled. Some preparation for the group may be needed with members prior to the meeting time. A phone call or letter, taking a few moments to talk, can all open the gates for intimacy in the group.

Henri Nouwen has coined the phrase "wounded healer." It applies to Jesus, "wounded for our transgressions" who now offers forgiveness for our sins. It also applies to our Christian witness. Those wounded can best speak and, as a result, "heal" those who are similarly wounded. This is the power behind all the self-help groups. Alcoholics meet together, sharing common burdens. The codependent meet together healing common wounds. The small group leader would do well to keep the "wounded healer" concept in mind. To share a weakness is to bring healing to someone with a similar weakness. To communicate a trouble is to not only pique the interest of everyone with that trouble, or of those who have an association with someone with that trouble, but it is also to build a bond between you and them based on that shared trouble.

Small group leaders are shepherds in the sense of leading the way in sharing weaknesses, troubles, and doubts, but more important small group leaders are shepherds who get down on their hands and knees to nurture their sheep. Yes, a small group leader is not just another lost sheep; however, an effective small group leader knows how to become vulnerable and share in the troubles of the sheep. Like Jesus, who "did not regard equality with God as something to be exploited, but emptied himself, taking the form of a slave" (Phil. 2:6-7), so small group leaders must empty himself or herself to share their intimacies so that they may serve by paving the way to intimacy with the expression of their own weaknesses, fears, and doubts.

Referee

A referee's role in a game is to make sure that the game is played according to the rules and to make judgments based on those rules. The rules that govern a small group are relatively simple: confidentiality, participation by everyone, and support and encouragement for everything shared.

Everything shared by the group must be held in strict confidence. The quickest way to destroy not only your own group's ministry, but the entire church's small group ministry, is to betray a confidence. Confidentiality should be strongly emphasized by the small group leader and the centrality of confidentiality should be given in writing. It may be good to go so far as to have the participants sign a form stating that they understand the importance of confidentiality. Communicating the importance of confidentiality and periodically affirming its importance is the function of the small group leader. Confidentiality will be betrayed gradually, through offhand remarks. When the rule gets stretched, it is best to immediately bring the rule back into focus.

The second rule that must be enforced by the small group leader is that everyone should participate. Certainly participation will not be equal. Some will have much more to say at any given meeting than others. One participant should not be allowed to dominate every meeting, but at any given meeting, one participant may dominate given a crisis or personal need. The role of the small group leader as referee is to cut short the long-winded and to encourage the meek. It is usually good to have one or two questions in a small group meeting that everyone is given an opportunity to respond to. Even if they say, "I have nothing to say," which is an acceptable response, at least a response has been given. Further, someone who never contributes to the group is just as harmful as someone who dominates. A small group is like a living organism. Each member must contribute to the whole for there to be health. If one member refuses to contribute, it is like an open sore to the group body. If one dominates to the exclusion of others, it is like a cancer to the group body. The small group leader must act like a referee, promoting and even demanding everyone's participation for the sake of health.

Finally, the small group leader, as referee, must encourage the other members to support and encourage participation by everyone in their group. Self-disclosure! The good of a small group is self-disclosure. Anyone who takes the risk of showing a piece of himself, through self-disclosure, should be looked upon as giving a priceless gift to the group. All that the group members give to the group in disclosing themselves in honesty should be considered priceless and treated accordingly. The small group leader must lead by example in this role of supporter, and encourage every offering of self by every participant in the group. A comment, such as "Thank you for sharing that" or "That story means a lot to me" or "That thought is important for us all to hear" can set the supportive tone in the group.

A word of caution for the leader in the referee role of the small group. Leading must always be by example. Whether it is confidentiality, the participation of everyone, or support and encouragement for everything shared, a small group leader is still a servant leader who leads primarily by example and not simply by enforcing the rules. Approach the process with humility. Recognize that words often betray meaning and often things are not as they sound or appear. These miscommunications can often be humorous. A family forms a small group in which we often must take a leadership role. Once, a child did not want to go to Pizza Hut when everyone else was in agreement. In trying to convince the child, about six years old at the time, of the virtues of eating pizza at Pizza Hut, the father made the statement, "Son, the pizza at Pizza Hut is probably the best pizza you'll ever eat in your short, but whole life." The boy looked at his father with contempt in his eyes and said indignantly, "Dad, don't call me a butt hole." The father repeated his son's accusation to himself, not believing his ears. "A butt hole, I didn't call him a butt hole." So to himself he repeated his statement. "Son, this is the best pizza you'll ever eat in your short, *but whole* life. Oh no, his son thought he said 'your short butt hole life' when he said 'your short, but whole life.'" He tried to explain. "Son, I didn't say this would be the best pizza in your '*short butt hole life*,' I said, this would be the best pizza in your 'short, but whole life,' meaning your entire life. Do you understand, son?" The son replied, "Yeah, you're saying I'm gonna be a butt hole my whole life."

This story illustrates that words do not always convey the true meaning of a statement. The resulting confusion can be humorous, or it can be deadly to the relationship. This can happen more often than we care to admit. Treat verbal communication with caution. Practice active listening by parroting back what someone has said. Make people restate their thoughts. The more a leader explores the meaning of the spoken words of a group, the more depth and intimacy in communication will be facilitated. Get below the surface. There is always more there than the initial words can convey.

Environmentalist

The final role of the small group leader is that of "environmentalist." Here I am speaking of the actual physical arrangement in the room where a small group meeting is being held. Use this checklist:

(1) Can everyone see one another? How is the lighting?
(2) Can everyone hear one another? Are there distracting noises?
(3) Is the seating uncomfortable?
(4) Is the seating too comfortable, more conducive to sleep than discussion?
(5) How is the room temperature?
(6) Is the seating just enough for the size of your group? Gaps in the seating that create a feeling of distance.
(7) Food and drinks offer a positive element to the atmosphere as long as they are served informally.
(8) How about a candle to set in the middle of the group for a time of prayer?
(9) How about music to sing with or listen to, to set the mood or atmosphere?

The small group leader must be the one who is sensitive to the group's setting in all its dynamics. When I work with youth and someone is lying down at a small group, I will ask them to sit up. A sleepy posture can create an air of unimportance and boredom that can easily infect the whole group.

A small group leader must be aware of unusual and distracting habits of the participants, not least of which is the bad habit of conversations on the side and off the subject. Draw these people back to the group as a whole with love, but firmness. Once, a girl in a group constantly cracked her knuckles. She was asked to stop. She was not even aware of the habit.

Covet the intimacy of your group. It can be easily compromised by "environmental" distraction that must be corrected as soon as possible for the sake of the group.

Leadership with Authority

Leadership with authority is most often large group leadership, but for our purposes, it is leadership that is opposite servant leadership. Compare the lists:

Servant Leadership	Authority Leadership
Of the heart	Of the head
Based on vulnerability	Based on expertise
Listens before talking	Talks before listening
Leads by example	Leads by talent and expertise
Ideal for small groups	Ideal for large groups
Offers support	Offers direction
Flexible	Predetermined
Weak	Strong
Many needed for the health of the whole	Few needed for the health of the whole
Open to the new	Prepackaged before delivery
Motivated by sensitivity	Motivated by benevolence
Creates questions	Creates answers
Motivating	Inspiring
Lots of gray	Much more black and white
Holds back	Assertive
Warm feeling	Excited feeling
Shares	Gives
Peaceful	Energized
Engaging	Entertaining

Leadership with authority is a necessary element within a healthy congregation; however, leadership with authority will not be developed as much as it will need to be identified. You do not need to teach leadership with authority to those who do not have it. Few leaders of this type are needed in a healthy church. In fact, most churches will find they have too many leaders of this type. The saying, "Too many Chiefs and not enough Indians" points out this potential problem; however, once identified, leaders with authority do need to develop a small group leader's attitude. A chief with a heart for the Indians is a powerful leader indeed. Jesus spoke as one with authority, but he also came to serve and not be served. The same is true of a servant leader or a small group leader. It would be helpful for a servant leader to develop the skills or the feel for a leader of authority.

A small group leader who is caring, but tough, listens, but is directed, is open, but not wishy-washy, will be a powerful small group leader indeed. For example, a small group leader wants to listen to the group, but if one member of the group dominates, on the one hand, and another member of the group fails to participate, on the other, both situations must be corrected with a more authoritarian direction. Let me give an example. A first grader has spelling words every week. She was taught to spell phonetically. She sounds out the word and spells the word accordingly. Unfortunately, phonics will not be a help in spelling every word. Some words break the phonetic rules. The first grader did not know her spelling words for the week. The truth was that she knew how the words were to be spelled, but she refused to spell the words correctly because they did not follow her phonetic rules. The word in question was "began." She explained that we do not say "began," we say "bi-gun" and so she spelled "began" *B I G U N*. She was told that her teacher did not care how we pronounced the word, "we" should spell it correctly. She refused. If you did not realize it by now, this six-year-old is gifted as a leader with authority. It was impossible for the teacher to deal with this first grader as a servant leader. Only a leader with authority can successfully correct another leader with authority. Later this student's family decided to go to Target, a modern general store. The first grader wanted to spend money she received at Christmas. It was the leverage her parents needed. She was told that all the children of this family must finish their homework before they could do anything else. Therefore, she had to spell her words correctly if she wanted to go. She refused. One parent stayed home with the daughter as she cried and pouted and stomped around the house. About fifteen minutes went by and she slapped a piece of paper in front of her parent and exclaimed, "I'll spell the words, but they're not right." Sure enough, she spelled all her words correctly on the first attempt, including the word "began."

A Time and Place

There is a time and place for everything, and there is a time and place for the two types of leadership. Even though, generally speaking, a large group or a governing body is a place for authoritarian leadership, still, a timely element of servant leadership is not only desirable but sometimes vital. On the other hand, generally speaking, a small group is a place for servant leadership to dominate. Still, there are times when a servant leader must take an authoritarian role. The family in general operates best under servant leadership. The family is a small group. Still, as outlined above, there are key instances when parental authority must be exercised for the health of the family. A general rule of parenting would be that the smaller the child, the more authoritarian parenting is needed, and the older the child, the more servant parenting is needed. Blessed is the parent who is wise in using both parenting styles.

A leader with authority can be an inspiring preacher, a talented entertainer, a knowledgeable teacher, a powerful example or witness. This leadership style grabs people's attention and captivates them. This leader makes a presentation that covers an audience like a net and takes them places they never dreamed of going. This is a charismatic gift in the truest sense of the word. A gift from God is to speak to the hearts and minds of a diverse group of people and draw on common elements to bring them together in spirit more than they can be brought together by any other means.

Often, a leader with authority is also a visionary. It is one thing to have the talent to bring people together in spirit, but it is another thing to take the people in a direction that is good and healthy. Obviously, this leadership can be good or bad. Some may use the talent to pervert rather than redeem. However, where a vision of goodness is the goal, the goal often can only be reached through the charisma of an authoritarian leader. This leader is willing to take risks. Failure is seen only as a necessary obstacle on the road to success. This is leadership that sees beyond the immediate. Seeing things as they are, but only as a jumping-off point for what can be and what should be. This leadership needs to be thick-skinned at best, able to take criticism. If this authoritarian leadership cannot take criticism, they will become defensive and even combative. It is leadership gone bad. Good authoritarian leadership sees the big picture, gets to the core, and passes by the insignificant. Finally, this leadership is able to make accurate assessments and evaluations. Not moved by diverse opinions and emotions, leadership with authority sees, evaluates, proposes direction, and sets off to conquer, often all within a moment's time. This is a gut feeling evaluation, not an evaluation based on surveys and interviews. The leader with authority thrives in acting alone. Someone once described a leadership style as inviting people to grab onto a towrope behind a speeding boat with the only instructions being, "Hang On." That describes authoritarian leadership.

The risks of this leadership style are threefold: burnout, the messiah complex, and insensitivity to the people led. Often an authoritarian leader goes one hundred miles per hour. This leader thinks everything is dependent upon him. This leader keeps going even when all the supports are gone. An authoritarian leader must be corrected by an equal or greater authority. This leader must be told to take care of himself, take breaks, slow down, don't work so hard, and that's an order. The authoritarian leader who cannot rest will burn out. "People can't drink from an empty cup." This truth must be hammered into this type of leader or they will literally kill themselves.

Another risk of being an authoritarian leader is developing a messianic complex. In the church, this messianic self-absorption is idolatry and a great harm to the church's work. It has been said that you can tell who the really great pastors are after they leave their churches. Does the church continue to flourish? If so, that church's messiah is Jesus the Christ. However, a church will suffer after a pastor leaves inasmuch as that church's messiah was the pastor rather than Jesus the Christ. It is the greatest temptation of a pastor to be the messiah rather than leading others to the Messiah. This is true for any leader with authority. All true authority comes from God, and where a leader becomes the source of authority, idolatry enters in and destruction will result.

The final risk of leadership with authority is insensitivity to the people led. Once a secretary criticized a business administrator as "an authority freak." She meant that this administrator acted and reacted without sensitivity to others. This is leadership by tyranny. It leads to resentment and mutiny.

Most church leaders must be skilled in both leadership styles. Perhaps the business world can survive with leadership that is only authoritarian, but a church will struggle under this leadership style alone. There can be compensating factors. A pastoral staff that has both leaders of authority and servant leaders can work effectively. A pastor may be authoritarian whose spouse or secretary can compensate by being the ears and heart for a strict authoritarian style. It would be best to teach the authoritarian leader the value and skills of a servant leader, just as it would be best to teach a servant leader authoritarian skills. This is true of every leadership position in the church. The important point to make is that more leaders need to be identified and trained in every church. A church without leaders goes nowhere. Leadership is both a gift to be identified and a skill to be learned. Leadership, leadership, leadership, is the only future our church has. Some of the possible directions the church of the future must take are outlined in the previous chapters, but leadership will be the necessary tool to accomplish the direction, whatever it may be.

At a recent worship service, the pastor began the service and simultaneously an annoying sound permeated the sanctuary. Was the sound system again possessed by the evil one? No! Not this time.

It was difficult to place, but it was evident that the sound was coming from an older woman's hearing aid. No one who sat near her responded. If anything, they inched farther away from her, repelled by the noise.

The pastor did not want to preach through the noise, so he got up at the hymn and sat next to her. He simply told her that her hearing aid was not working properly and needed to be turned down.

Many who have been faithful to the church of the past century and, perhaps, the churches themselves, have developed hearing problems. We are in need of hearing aids. If the faithful continue to close their ears to the new sounds of God's spirit, everyone will suffer.

You can be that hearing aid. You can help your church step into the next century, hearing clearly the voices now calling out, and you can help to take away the annoying sounds from instruments designed to assist in hearing, but are now giving off only distracting noise.

Are you reaching new generations of believers? Romans 10:14 asks the questions, "But how are they to call on one in whom they have not believed? And how are they to believe in one of whom they have never heard? And how are they to hear without someone to proclaim him?" Leadership is your call to accomplish God's call to new generations of believers. God bless you in that effort.